Reading 2

Advantage

Second Edition

Casey Malarcher

THOMSON
™
HEINLE

Australia · Canada · Mexico · Singapore · Spain · United Kingdom · United States

THOMSON

HEINLE

Reading Advantage, *Second Edition*, Student Book 2

Casey Malarcher

Publisher, Global ELT: Christopher Wenger
Editorial Manager: Sean Bermingham
Development Editor: Derek Mackrell
Production Editor: Tan Jin Hock
ELT Directors: John Lowe (Asia), Jim Goldstone (Latin America—ELT), Francisco Lozano (Latin America—Academic and Training, ELT)

Director of Marketing, ESL/ELT: Amy Mabley
Marketing Manager: Ian Martin
Interior/Cover Design: Christopher Hanzie, TYA Inc.
Composition: Stella Tan and Ronn Lee, TYA Inc.
Cover Images: PhotoDisc, Inc.
Printer: Seng Lee Press

Printed in Singapore
3 4 5 6 7 8 9 10   07 06 05

For permission to use material from this text or product, contact us in the United States:
Tel   1-800-730-2214
Fax   1-800-730-2215
Web   www.thomsonrights.com

For more information, contact Heinle, 25 Thomson Place, Boston, Massachusetts 02210 USA, or you can visit our Internet site at http://www.heinle.com

ISBN 1-4130-0115-7

Credits

Unless otherwise stated, all photos are from PhotoDisc, Inc. Digital Imagery © copyright 2003 PhotoDisc, Inc. Photos on pages 28, 54, 79, and 80 are the exclusive property of Heinle. Photos on pages 6, 10, 21, 39, and 40 are from Associated Press. Photos from other sources: pages 9 and 62: © Index Stock; page 13: © Neal Preston/CORBIS; page 14: © Jan Butchofsky-Houser/CORBIS; page 18: © Starbucks Coffee Company; page 22: © CORBIS; page 27: © Douglas Peebles/CORBIS; pages 43 and 44: © Reuters NewMedia Inc./CORBIS; page 50: © Bettmann/CORBIS

Dictionary definitions are adapted from Heinle's *Newbury House Dictionary of American English*, © 2002, Monroe Allen Publishers, Inc.
Sources of information: www.guinnessworldrecords.com (Units 1, 3, 5, 7, and 14); *Sydney Morning Herald*, March 1, 2003, "Why the Queen's on the Money" and http://www.forbes.com/2003/02/26/billionaireland.html (Unit 1); http://www.ananova.com/news/story/sm_453621.html (Unit 2); *TIME Magazine*, June 4, 2001, "101 Pixels of Fun," http://www.businessweek.com/magazine/content/02_07/b3770009.htm, and http://www.morningindia.com/Education/carreerM.asp?OPT=JOCK (Unit 3); http://www.cdf.org/cdf/atissue/vol1_1/starbucks/starbucks.html and http://www.forbes.com/global/2002/0415/069.html (Unit 4); http://www.mariner.org/age/magellan.html, http://www.wikipedia.org/wiki/Elizabeth_Jane_Cochran, and http://home.earthlink.net/~earthwalker1/ (Unit 5); http://www.ultramarathonworld.com/uw_archive/n17se00e.html (Review 1–5); http://vm.cfsan.fda.gov/~mow/fugu.html (Unit 6); http://www.indiancountry.com/?2592 (Unit 7); http://news.bbc.co.uk/cbbcnews/hi/find_out/guides/2003/bollywood/ (Unit 9); http://www.nobel.se/ (Unit 10); http://www.pulitzer.org (Review 6–10); http://www.harvardsquarelibrary.org/unitarians/cousins.html (Unit 11); http://www.astropalmistry.com/chiromancy.html and http://www.psychrealm.com/palmfaq.htm (Unit 12); http://www.worldmemorychampionships.com, *Sydney Morning Herald*, December 16, 2002, "Ancient Greek Trick to Memory Feats," and http://www.pi-world-ranking-list.com/lists/details/tomoyori2.html (Unit 13); www.milleniumdog.freeserve.co.uk (Unit 14); *The Guardian*, February 19, 2002, "Gang in £200m Dome Diamond Raid Sent to Jail" and http://news.bbc.co.uk/2/hi/europe/2806161.stm (Unit 15); www.bbc.co.uk/crime/caseclosed/crimes.shtml (Review 11–15); http://www.space.com/missionlaunches/triumph_tragedy_030210-1.html, http://www.wikipedia.org/wiki/International_Space_Station, and charlottemason.tripod.com/winter.html (Unit 16); http://www.chariho.k12.ri.us/curriculum/MISmart/cultures/am_newyr.html and http://www.msc.edu.ph/wired/newyear.html (Unit 17); http://www.telegraph.co.uk/news/main.jhtml?xml=/news/2003/03/03/ntext03.xml, *The Australian*, May 29, 2003, "Saved by SMS," http://www.ananova.com/news/story/sm_681034.html (Unit 18); www.snopes.com and http://urbanlegends.about.com/library/blhairyarm.htm (Unit 19); http://www.hickoksports.com/history/xgames.shtml, http://www.bungee.com/bzapp/press/hrn.html, and http://abcnews.go.com/sections/wnt/WorldNewsTonight/LeeCam_landdivers_feature.html (Unit 20); www.wikipedia.org/mars_pathfinder (Review 16–20)

Contents

To the Teacher

Welcome to *Reading Advantage Book 2*! In this book, students will find readings and exercises to help build their English vocabulary and reading skills. Each of the units in this book is divided into seven parts. These parts are meant to be studied together to help students develop reading skills, as well as review new vocabulary and reinforce vocabulary presented in other units.

Before You Read

This part of each unit presents questions for students to think about before they read the passage. The questions focus on knowledge students already have on the subject of the passage, as well as questions which will be answered in the reading. Students may discuss (or write) the answers to these questions before reading.

Target Vocabulary

In this section, students are introduced to words from the reading that they may not know. Students should be able to match the words with the simple definitions provided. After studying these words, students may continue with the reading.

Reading Passage

Each reading passage in Book 2 is around 300 words in length. Students should first read this passage alone silently. At the end of each passage, the word count for the readings is shown, with a space for students to record their reading time for the passage. By keeping track of their reading times, using the chart inside the back cover of this book, students will be able to see the improvement in their reading speeds over the course. Each reading is recorded on the audio cassette/CD; after students have read through silently, they can listen to the passage narrated by a native English speaker.

Reading Comprehension

This section is a series of multiple-choice questions about the passage. Students are encouraged to look back at the reading in order to check their answers to these questions. The questions cover important reading skills, such as understanding the main idea, scanning for details, and reading for inference.

Idioms

This section highlights three idioms from the reading passage. The meaning of these idioms and examples of how they may be used are presented.

Vocabulary Reinforcement

This section is divided into two parts. Section A has six multiple-choice sentences for vocabulary and idiom practice. Section B presents a cloze passage with missing words which students need to complete using vocabulary items from the box. Vocabulary and idioms tested in this section have been selected from the present unit, as well as earlier units in the book.

What Do You Think?

Students are encouraged to think further about what they have read and communicate their own ideas and feelings about the topics presented. Answers to these questions can be used as a writing activity if desired.

There are also four review units in this book—one after every five units. Because each review unit tests vocabulary and idioms from the preceding five units, and later units recycle vocabulary from earlier ones, it is recommended that, where possible, units be completed in the order in which they are presented.

I hope both you and your students enjoy using *Reading Advantage*!

Casey Malarcher

Billionaires

Before You Read

Answer the following questions.

1. Who do you think is the wealthiest person in the world? _____

2. Who is the wealthiest person in your country?
   How did he or she become wealthy? _____

3. Do you know of any young people who are very rich? _____

Target Vocabulary

Match each word with the best meaning.

1. _____ determine   **a.** said

2. _____ personal   **b.** decide; choose

3. _____ property   **c.** not public; belonging to someone

4. _____ wealth   **d.** a large amount of money and property

5. _____ worth   **e.** things owned by someone

6. _____ nation   **f.** value or cost

7. _____ reported   **g.** decide or guess something, e.g., a number or price

8. _____ estimate   **h.** country

There are really two classes of wealthy people. Millionaires are rich. Billionaires are super rich! However, **determining** a person's **wealth** is not always easy.

The wealth of a king or queen, for example, is based on the wealth and **property** of the **nation** instead of the **personal** wealth and property of the king or queen.
5 For some kings and queens, it is difficult to tell these two kinds of wealth apart.

The richest member of a royal family is Prince Alwaleed Bin Talal Alsaud. His personal wealth was **estimated** in 2003 to be $18 billion. Her Majesty Queen
10 Elizabeth II is often thought to be the richest woman in the world. However, when the public property of England is ruled out, her personal money and property seem rather small. Queen Elizabeth II's
15 personal wealth was estimated in 2003 to be $397 million. This was less than J. K. Rowling, the author of the Harry Potter books, who was estimated to be **worth** $444 million.

20 In the United States, there were 222 people **reported** to be billionaires in 2003. The richest of these is Bill Gates, worth at least $41 billion, who made his money by starting the company Microsoft. Mr. Gates
25 was only twenty years old when he first helped to set up the company in 1976. He was a billionaire by the time he was thirty-one.

Mr. Gates may seem young to be so rich, but other people have made a lot of money at even younger ages. Other young people who have struck it rich include Jackie Coogan (1914–1984) and Shirley Temple (1928–). Both of these child
30 actors made over a million dollars acting in movies before they were fourteen years old. However, the youngest billionaire is Albert von Thurn und Taxis of Germany, who, in 2001, inherited[1] a billion dollars when he turned eighteen!

_____ **minutes** _____ **seconds** (315 words)

> ### Did You Know?
> The richest person ever was John D. Rockefeller, of America, who was worth $900 million in 1913. That would be the same as having $190 billion today!

---

[1] **inherit** receive from someone, usually a relative, after the person dies

Reading Comprehension

Circle the letter of the best answer.

1. What is the best title for this passage?
   - **a.** How to Become a Billionaire
   - **b.** The Life of Bill Gates
   - **c.** Wealthy People of the World
   - **d.** Child Billionaires

2. Why is determining a person's wealth sometimes difficult?
   - **a.** The difference between public and private property is sometimes unclear.
   - **b.** Some wealthy people are very young.
   - **c.** Kings and queens are very private people and keep their wealth hidden.
   - **d.** There are very few billionaires in the world.

3. According to this passage, who is the richest person in the world?
   - **a.** Prince Alwaleed Bin Talal Alsaud
   - **b.** Queen Elizabeth II
   - **c.** J. K. Rowling
   - **d.** Bill Gates

4. In what year did Bill Gates become a billionaire?
   - **a.** 1956
   - **b.** 1976
   - **c.** 1987
   - **d.** 2003

5. Which of these people did not have to work for their money?
   - **a.** J. K. Rowling
   - **b.** Bill Gates
   - **c.** Jackie Coogan
   - **d.** Albert von Thurn und Taxis

Idioms

Find each idiom in the story.

1. **rule out**—*decide something is not possible*
   - Our high school lost the game, so we have been **ruled out** of the finals.
   - Who stole the money? Well, Lance was with his parents, so we can **rule him out**.

2. **strike it rich**—*become rich quickly*
   - John's uncle **struck it rich** through his online business.
   - Sarah thinks she can **strike it rich** by gambling in Las Vegas.

3. **make money**—*earn money*
   - I **made some money** by working over the summer.
   - Ray sold his house and **made a lot of money**.

Vocabulary Reinforcement

A. Circle the letter of the word or phrase that best completes the sentence.

1. There are _____ to be six billion people in the world.

   a. determined   **b.** earned   **c.** estimated   **d.** told

2. Last night, the news _____ an earthquake in Turkey.

   a. reported   **b.** said   **c.** told   **d.** estimated

3. So many good people applied for the job that it's hard to _____ anyone.

   a. make money   **b.** rule out   **c.** estimate   **d.** report

4. His house is thought to be _____ $20 million.

   a. worth   **b.** value   **c.** cost   **d.** property

5. Thirty-two _____ compete in the soccer World Cup tournament.

   a. kings   **b.** public   **c.** personal   **d.** nations

6. I think that being an actor would be a fun way to _____ money.

   a. report   **b.** make   **c.** inherit   **d.** estimate

B. Complete the passage with items from the box. One item is extra.

estimated struck it rich personal wealth worth determine

It is not easy to (1)_____ how rich kings and queens are. The wealth of a king
or queen comes from the person's (2)_____ property or from money and
property of the nation. Looking at personal wealth, a Saudi Arabian prince is probably
the richest royal, (3)_____ to be worth $18 billion. But Bill Gates is richer. He
(4)_____ with his computer company Microsoft, and all of his property and
money is (5)_____ $41 billion.

What Do You Think?

1. If you were a billionaire, how would you spend your money?

2. What advice would you give to someone who wanted to become a billionaire?

Andre Agassi 2

Answer the following questions.

1. Do you like watching or playing tennis? Is the sport popular in your country?

_____

_____

2. What kind of qualities do you think someone needs to become a professional tennis player?

_____

_____

3. What do you know about the tennis player Andre Agassi?

_____

_____

■ Target Vocabulary

Match each word with the best meaning.

1. _____ afraid

2. _____ achievement

3. _____ despite

4. _____ career

5. _____ hairstyle

6. _____ refuse

7. _____ determination

8. _____ victory

a. say no

b. a win

c. strong mind or willpower

d. life's work, especially in business or a job

e. scared; frightened

f. although

g. the way someone's hair is cut

h. something someone has succeeded in doing, usually after a lot of work

When thirty-two-year-old tennis player Andre Agassi made it to the final of the U.S. Clay Court Championship[1] in April 2003, he set a new world record: he became the oldest player ever to be
5 number one in the world's tennis rankings.[2] It was one of the greatest **achievements** in Agassi's long and successful career.

Andre Agassi turned professional in 1986 at the age of sixteen. His **career** soon took off, and in
10 1990, he reached the finals of both the U.S. Open and the French Open championships.

By the age of twenty, Agassi was famous around the world, **despite** never having won an important tennis championship. Many people thought he was
15 famous more for his long blond hair and colorful tennis shirts than for his tennis skills. They wondered if he could really win an important tournament.

In 1992, Agassi proved these people wrong by winning one of the greatest prizes in world tennis—the Wimbledon singles[3] final. His first attempt to win this tournament had been in 1987, but he lost his opening game. He then **refused** to
20 take part at Wimbledon for the next three years. He said his reason for not playing was that the officials refused to allow him to wear his colorful shirts, but some people said it was because he was **afraid** to lose.

After several more championship **victories**, Agassi's luck began to run out. By 1997, the year of his marriage to movie actress Brooke Shields, Agassi's ranking
25 had dropped to 141st in the world. Many people thought his career was over.

Agassi and Shields divorced two years later, and Agassi made a comeback with a new trainer, a new **hairstyle**, and new **determination**. In 1999, he won both the French Open and the U.S. Open and ended the year back as the world's number one. By 2003, he had earned more than $27 million in prize money, making him
30 one of the most successful tennis players of all time.

✊ _____ **minutes** _____ **seconds** (329 words)

> ### Did You Know?
> In October 2001, Agassi married German tennis star Steffi Graf and they later had a baby son. For his birthday their son was given twenty-one small tennis rackets!

---

[1] **Clay Court Championship** a tournament played on a tennis court made from clay (a hard material also commonly used to make pots and plates)
[2] **ranking** an ordered list of people or places
[3] **singles** match where one player plays another player; in doubles, two teams of two players play against each other

Reading Comprehension

Circle the letter of the best answer.

1. What is the best title for this passage?

    a. An Amazing Career

    b. The World's Oldest Tennis Player

    c. A Celebrity Marriage and Divorce

    d. Great Championship Matches

2. How old was Agassi when he won his first championship?

    a. sixteen

    b. twenty

    c. twenty-two

    d. thirty-two

3. Who are "these people" in "Agassi proved these people wrong . . ." (line 17)?

    a. people who beat Agassi in tennis matches

    b. people who thought Agassi could not win a championship

    c. Brooke Shields and other movie actresses

    d. other ranked tennis players

4. When did Agassi and Shields divorce?

    a. 1995

    b. 1997

    c. 1999

    d. 2003

5. Which of these did NOT happen to Agassi in 1999?

    a. He got divorced.

    b. He won the French Open.

    c. He finished at number one in the rankings.

    d. He won $27 million.

Idioms

Find each idiom in the story.

1. **prove (someone) wrong**—*show that someone is wrong*
    - They thought I couldn't do it, but I **proved them wrong**.
    - Sarah **proved her parents wrong** by getting a part in the movie.

2. **run out (of something)**—*use all of something*
    - Could you get some milk at the shop? We've **run out**.
    - We've **run out of** paper for the photocopier. We need to buy some more.

3. **make a comeback**—*return to the top level of success*
    - Everyone thought her singing career was over, but she **made a comeback**.
    - He **made a comeback** after not starring in a movie for fifteen years.

Vocabulary Reinforcement

A. Circle the letter of the word or phrase that best completes the sentence.

1. I couldn't finish the exam because I _____ time.
   a. finished   **b.** lost   **c.** ran out of   **d.** estimated

2. Graduating from university was a great _____ for her.
   a. achievement   **b.** career   **c.** determination   **d.** wealth

3. My mother is really _____ of spiders.
   a. dislike   **b.** refused   **c.** afraid   **d.** hate

4. The main reason for his success is his strong _____.
   a. victory   **b.** achievement   **c.** career   **d.** determination

5. Everyone thought she wouldn't succeed, but she _____.
   a. showed them off   **b.** proved them wrong   **c.** ran out of them   **d.** turned their attention to it

6. Her grandfather has just retired after a long and successful _____.
   a. career   **b.** hairstyle   **c.** victory   **d.** achievement

B. Complete the passage with items from the box. One item is extra.

achievement victory career determination comeback run out

Andre Agassi began his (1)_____ as a professional tennis player when he was a teenager. His first big (2)_____ was in 1992 at Wimbledon. After winning several more championships, his luck seemed to (3)_____. For several years he did not play well, and his ranking fell to 141. Then in 1999, he made a (4)_____ with a new trainer and a new look. In 2003, he became the oldest player to be ranked number one in the world at tennis. It was the greatest (5)_____ of his career so far.

What Do You Think?

1. Do you know of any other famous people who have made comebacks? How did they make their comeback?

2. Do you think the Wimbledon officials were right to refuse to allow Agassi to play because of his clothing? What do you think about rules that determine what people can wear?

Video Jockeys 3

Before You Read

Answer the following questions.

1. The people pictured above are video jockeys (VJs). Do you know what VJs do? How are they different from DJs? _____

2. How many music video channels are on TV in your country? _____

3. How often do you watch music videos on television? _____

Target Vocabulary

Match each word with the best meaning.

1. _____ alternative
2. _____ channel
3. _____ material
4. _____ equipment
5. _____ in addition
6. _____ variety
7. _____ viewer
8. _____ content

a. person watching a show
b. a TV station
c. another choice; (adj.) unusual
d. what something is made of
e. tools or machines
f. many different choices
g. also; and
h. things contained inside something; (for TV or radio) programs and songs

13

DJs (disc jockeys) are the people who play and present music on the radio, or in a nightclub. A VJ (video jockey) is a person who introduces music videos on television.

5 VJs were first seen on television in the early 1980s when MTV went on the air. As MTV caught on, and the audience for music videos expanded, a **variety** of other music video **channels** started broadcasting. **In addition** to 10 rock music, there were channels for people who were into **alternative** kinds of music, such as country music, light rock, and R & B,[1] and all of these channels needed VJs. By the 15 1990s, international music video channels like Channel V in Asia and VIVA in Europe had started.

The VJs for the new international stations had to be chosen carefully. Although some VJs did shows focused on 20 small audiences and showed mostly local **content**, other VJs presented shows for international **viewers**. These VJs, and the **material** they presented, needed to be popular in several different cultures.

One successful international VJ in Asia is Asha Gill. She is from Malaysia, but her parents and grandparents are from India, France, and England. She speaks three 25 languages and has fans across Asia, from Japan to the United Arab Emirates.

Another VJ who has made a big hit in Asia is Lili. She is actually a computer-animated[2] VJ on MTV Asia. An actress wearing special computer **equipment** makes Lili move like a puppet.[3] The actress also talks for Lili, and her shows can be seen in five languages.

30 When asked what makes a good video jockey, many successful VJs have given similar answers. To be a good VJ you need to know a lot about music, you need to be funny, and you can't be shy.

_____ **minutes** _____ **seconds** (294 words)

Did You Know?

The most expensive music video ever filmed was 1995's _Scream_ by Michael and Janet Jackson. It cost $7 million to make!

---

[1] **R & B** rhythm and blues
[2] **computer-animated** drawn using a computer
[3] **puppet** a toy person you move by pulling strings, or by putting your hand inside it

Reading Comprehension

Circle the letter of the best answer.

1. What is the reading mainly about?

   a. how to become a VJ

   b. the most popular VJ today

   c. the differences between DJs and VJs

   d. some general information about VJs

2. What kind of music did the first VJ probably introduce?

   a. classical

   b. country

   c. rhythm and blues

   d. rock and pop

3. What do Channel V and VIVA have in common?

   a. They are both owned by MTV.

   b. They are music video channels in Asia.

   c. They do not use VJs to introduce the music.

   d. They have viewers in more than one country.

4. Which is NOT true about Asha Gill?

   a. She speaks more than one language

   b. Her family were all born in Malaysia.

   c. She's popular in quite a lot of Asian countries.

   d. She is a successful VJ.

5. Which of the following does the passage NOT mention as being important for someone who wants to be a VJ?

   a. speak many different languages

   b. listen to a lot of music

   c. talk easily with different people

   d. being able to make people laugh

Idioms

Find each idiom in the story.

1. **on the air**—*broadcast on TV or radio*
   - It's too early to turn on the TV. None of the channels are **on the air** yet.
   - The radio station went **off the air** after the owner died.

2. **catch on**—*become popular*
   - I think this new song will really **catch on**.
   - The new fashion quickly **caught on**, and soon everyone was wearing it.

3. **be into something**—*have a lot of interest in something*
   - He's really **into** cars and motorbikes.
   - She loves going to bookstores, but she's not really **into** clothes shopping.

Vocabulary Reinforcement

A. Circle the letter of the word or phrase that best matches the words in *italics.*

1. She didn't like the show, so she changed the *station.*

   a. event   **b.** title   **c.** channel   **d.** wealth

2. This store sells a bigger *variety* of products than other stores.

   a. choice   **b.** total   **c.** alternative   **d.** worth

3. Most of the *viewers* of the program are teenage girls.

   a. audience   **b.** property   **c.** makers   **d.** variety

4. Her brother is *interested in* chatting online.

   a. about   **b.** with   **c.** into   **d.** by

5. The *story* of this movie is not for children.

   a. career   **b.** content   **c.** channel   **d.** viewer

6. My sister is really into *alternative* movies.

   a. unusual   **b.** common   **c.** dangerous   **d.** afraid

B. Complete the passage with items from the box. One item is extra.

material   caught on   in addition   on the air   viewers   a variety of

Music video channels first went (1)_____ in the 1980s, and quickly
(2)_____. These channels used (3)_____ people called VJs to introduce
the music videos. International music video channels try to find VJs and (4)_____
to fit a wide audience. Channels like Channel V and VIVA have (5)_____ from
many countries.

What Do You Think?

1. What is your favorite channel on television? Why do you like it?

2. Have you seen any TV programs made in another country? Which ones? What did you
think of them?

Coffee Culture 4

Before You Read

Answer the following questions.

1. How often do you drink coffee?
   Where and when do you drink it?

2. Is coffee popular in your country?
   If not, what other drinks are popular?

3. Are there any Starbucks coffee shops in your area?
   What do you know about this company?

Target Vocabulary

Match each word with the best meaning.

1. _____ atmosphere
2. _____ location
3. _____ roast
4. _____ casual
5. _____ run (something)
6. _____ create
7. _____ downtown
8. _____ hire

a. cook using dry heat, or in an oven

b. give someone a job

c. manage (e.g., a company)

d. make something for the first time

e. place; where something is

f. the center of a city

g. the feeling created by furniture, lights, music, etc.

h. relaxed; not formal

The first Starbucks coffee shop opened in 1971 in **downtown** Seattle, Washington, in the United States. It was a small coffee shop that **roasted** its own
5 coffee beans. The coffee shop's business did well, and by 1981 there were three more Starbucks stores in Seattle.

Things really began to <u>c</u>hange for the company in 1981. That year, Howard
10 Schultz met the three men who **ran** Starbucks. Schultz worked in New York for a company that made kitchen equipment. He noticed that Starbucks ordered a large number of special coffee makers, and he was curious about the company. Schultz went to Seattle to see what Starbucks did, and he liked what he saw. He
15 wanted to become part of the company. In 1982, the original Starbucks owners **hired** Schultz as the company's head of marketing.[1]

In 1983, Schultz traveled to Italy. The unique **atmosphere** of the espresso[2] bars there caught his eye. To Schultz it seemed that Italians spent their daily lives in three places: home, work, and coffee bars. His experience in Italy gave Schultz a
20 new idea for Starbucks back in Seattle.

Schultz **created** an atmosphere for Starbucks coffee shops that was comfortable and **casual**, and customers everywhere seemed to like it. Between 1987 and 1992, Starbucks opened 150 new stores—and that was only the beginning. As a matter of fact, by the year 2000, three new Starbucks stores opened somewhere around
25 the world every day!

Today, Starbucks has thousands of stores, including stores in twenty-six countries. One thing that helps make Starbucks succeed in cities outside the United States is the way Starbucks works with local stores and restaurants. By working together with a store already in the city, Starbucks gains an understanding of customers in
30 the city. This understanding helps Starbucks open stores in the right **locations** for their customers.

 _____ **minutes** _____ **seconds** (305 words)

---

[1] **marketing** the job of selling a product, planning advertising, deciding prices, and so on
[2] **espresso** a small cup of strong, black coffee

Reading Comprehension

Circle the letter of the best answer.

1. What is the main topic of the reading?

   a. how Starbucks has grown

   b. what Starbucks makes

   c. Starbucks' customers

   d. how Starbucks makes its coffee

2. Which is true about Starbucks' first ten years of business?

   a. It grew very quickly.

   b. It was run by Howard Schultz.

   c. It was a small company.

   d. It made special coffee makers.

3. Who is Howard Schultz?

   a. a coffee seller from New York

   b. an Italian coffee maker

   c. the man who changed the company

   d. one of the original owners of the company

4. About how many new Starbucks opened in 1999?

   a. 3

   b. 150

   c. 300

   d. more than 1,000

5. What helps Starbucks succeed in places outside the United States?

   a. opening restaurants in just a few locations each year

   b. only selling locally produced coffee beans

   c. working with other major coffee-making companies

   d. learning about local customers

Idioms

Find each idiom in the story.

1. **catch one's eye**—*attract one's attention; make one see or notice*
   - While we were window shopping, this dress **caught my eye**.
   - They wanted the ad to **catch the eye** of readers.

2. **gain an understanding**—*learn about; get to know something about*
   - This class will help you **gain an understanding** of how computers work.
   - They both **gained an understanding** of each other from the experience.

3. **as a matter of fact**—*in fact; actually*
   - I read your homework. I have it here on my desk, **as a matter of fact**.
   - She's leaving the country. **As a matter of fact**, she's flying to Paris tomorrow.

Vocabulary Reinforcement

A. Circle the letter of the word or phrase that best matches the words in *italics*.

1. The bright lights *caught his eye.*
   a. made him look   b. scared him   c. saw him   d. upset him

2. Put the meat in the oven and *roast* it for two hours.
   a. eat   b. cook   c. serve   d. hire

3. She didn't think the newspaper's *content* was very interesting.
   a. ending   b. atmosphere   c. information   d. equipment

4. I don't know how to use the new office *equipment.*
   a. channels   b. events   c. machines   d. locations

5. The meeting yesterday was very *casual.*
   a. mixed   b. new   c. professional   d. relaxed

6. My uncle owns *property* in the country.
   a. land   b. location   c. atmosphere   d. downtown

B. Complete the passage with items from the box. One item is extra.

atmosphere   created   downtown   equipment   as a matter of fact   hired

Starbucks began as a small coffee company in (1)_____ Seattle in the United States. A man in New York noticed the small company bought a lot of special (2)_____ to make coffee. He went to Seattle to learn about the company and was later (3)_____ by Starbucks. This man changed the (4)_____ of the stores and helped to make Starbucks a huge company. (5)_____, Starbucks today has thousands of stores in more than twenty different countries.

What Do You Think?

1. Starbucks coffee shops are popular places for young people to meet and "hang out" with friends. Where do you and your friends like to meet? Why do you choose those places?

2. Is there a company from your country that has been successful internationally? What do you think are the reasons for its success?

Around the World 5

Before You Read

Answer the following questions.

1. Do you know any people who are famous for exploring or traveling?

_____

_____

2. Are there any famous explorers from your country?

_____

_____

3. In 2002, Steve Fossett (pictured on the left) succeeded in doing something no one else had done before. What do you think it was?

_____

_____

Target Vocabulary

Match each word with the best meaning.

1. _____ article
2. _____ author
3. _____ eventually
4. _____ explorer
5. _____ journalist
6. _____ novel
7. _____ theory
8. _____ trip

a. a person who goes to new places to learn about them
b. a journey
c. in the end; finally
d. a scientific idea
e. writer of books, articles, etc.
f. a fictional book
g. newspaper or magazine writer
h. newspaper or magazine story

For most of human history, people thought the world was flat. That is, they thought that if you traveled far enough in one direction, you would **eventually** come to the edge of the world. Then, about two thousand years ago, people started to come up with the **theory** that the earth was round. This meant that by
5 traveling far enough in a straight line, you would eventually come back to where you started.

Ferdinand Magellan

It wasn't until the sixteenth century that Ferdinand Magellan's expedition[1] became the first to travel around the world. The expedition first sailed west from
10 Portugal, around South America, across the Pacific, before returning around South Africa back to Portugal. Although Magellan died during the voyage, one of his captains, Sebastian del Cano, made it all the way.

In 1872, the French science fiction **author** Jules
15 Verne published a book called *Around the World in 80 Days*. The **novel** was about a man who travels around the world, starting from London, to win a bet.

In 1889, an American **journalist**, Nellie Bly, was sent by her newspaper to complete the journey taken by the characters in Verne's book. She traveled around
20 the world, sending **articles** back to her newspaper about her journey. She finally arrived back home after her **trip**, taking 72 days, six hours, eleven minutes, and fourteen seconds to go around the world.

Even though traveling around the world these days is very easy, and can be done in one or two days by plane, people are still interested in breaking records.

25 From 1970 to 1974, an American, Dave Kunst, was the first person to walk all the way around the world. He wore out twenty-one pairs of shoes on his trip! The first airplane flight around the world took place in 1924, completed by Lt.[2] Lowell H. Smith and five other American pilots, and the first solo helicopter flight around the world was done by an Australian **explorer**, Dick Smith, in
30 1982–83.

As for a nonstop balloon flight all the way around the world, this wasn't completed until 2002, when Steve Fossett eventually succeeded after many attempts.

_____ **minutes** _____ **seconds** (353 words)

Did You Know?
An American couple, Robert and Carmen Becker, are the most traveled couple in the world. There are only six areas on Earth they haven't visited.

---

[1] **expedition** a scientific or adventurous journey
[2] **Lt.** Lieutenant (a military officer rank)

Reading Comprehension

Circle the letter of the best answer.

1. Who first said that the world was not flat?
   - **a.** Ferdinand Magellan
   - **b.** Jules Verne
   - **c.** Nellie Bly
   - **d.** The passage doesn't say.

2. Which of these people did NOT go on a journey around the world?
   - **a.** Ferdinand Magellan
   - **b.** Jules Verne
   - **c.** Nellie Bly
   - **d.** Steve Fossett

3. What did Jules Verne and Nellie Bly have in common?
   - **a.** They both traveled around the world.
   - **b.** They were both American.
   - **c.** They both wrote about traveling around the world.
   - **d.** They were both journalists.

4. Which is NOT true about David Kunst's journey?
   - **a.** He wore out a lot of shoes.
   - **b.** He took four years to complete it.
   - **c.** He traveled through twenty-one countries.
   - **d.** He set a world record.

5. Which of these people did NOT travel around the world by air?
   - **a.** Nellie Bly
   - **b.** Lowell H. Smith
   - **c.** Dick Smith
   - **d.** Steve Fossett

Idioms

Find each idiom in the story.

1. **even though**—*although; despite (the fact that)*
   - We decided to go on our picnic, **even though** it looked like it would rain.
   - I passed the exam, **even though** I didn't study.

2. **wear out**—*make something useless by using it too much*
   - I need to get new tires for my car. The old ones are completely **worn out**.
   - The carpet on the stairs is **worn out** from people walking on it.

3. **these days**—*now (but not in the past)*
   - **These days**, young people are waiting longer to get married.
   - People have no manners **these days**.

Vocabulary Reinforcement

A. Circle the letter of the word or phrase that best completes the sentence.

1. I read a great _____ in the newspaper this morning.
   a. article   **b.** novel   **c.** journalist   **d.** author

2. I waited for about thirty minutes before the bus _____ came.
   a. explorer   **b.** reported   **c.** eventually   **d.** in addition

3. Have a great _____! See you next week.
   a. explorer   **b.** trip   **c.** theory   **d.** novel

4. She has a very interesting _____ about what happened to the dinosaurs.
   a. explorer   **b.** journalist   **c.** location   **d.** theory

5. After I graduate I'd like to get a job as a newspaper _____.
   a. journalist   **b.** author   **c.** article   **d.** program

6. He has written three prize-winning _____.
   a. authors   **b.** journalists   **c.** novels   **d.** materials

B. Complete the passage with items from the box. One item is extra.

author	explorer	wore out	even though	these days	eventually

(1)_____ it's very easy to travel around the world, but it wasn't always like this.
The first expedition to go all the way around the world was led by the (2)_____
Ferdinand Magellan, in the sixteenth century. (3)_____ you can easily fly around
the world now, people are still interested in breaking records. One man walked around the
world. His trip took four years before he (4)_____ finished, and he
(5)_____ twenty-one pairs of shoes!

What Do You Think?

1. If you could have gone on one of the journeys mentioned in the passage, which one
   would you like to have joined? Why?

2. If you were going to travel around the world, where would you go? How would you
   travel?

Review

A. Find words for each definition. Two words are extra.

alternative	atmosphere	author	channel	content	create
determine	in addition	location	material	property	victory

1. _____ a TV station
2. _____ a win
3. _____ also; and
4. _____ another choice; unusual
5. _____ decide; choose
6. _____ make something for the first time
7. _____ place; where something is
8. _____ things contained inside something
9. _____ things owned by someone
10. _____ what something is made of

B. Complete the paragraph with items from the box. Two items are extra.

achievement	afraid	alternative	despite	determination	equipment
estimates	even though	eventually	proved them wrong	ruled out	running out

The first woman to walk around the world was a young British woman named Ffyona Campbell. Between 1983 and 1994, Ffyona walked across Europe, the United States, Africa, and Australia. She (1)_____ that she walked 31,519 kilometers. Some people thought she wouldn't be able to do it, but she (2)_____. She says it was hard work, and took a lot of (3)_____. "A few times I had to reach very deep inside to find something to keep me going," she said.

(4)_____ her great (5)_____ Ffyona wasn't happy. She had a secret, and (6)_____ she had to tell it to people. During her walk across America, she was (7)_____ her strength was (8)_____, and so she decided to ride in the car that was carrying her (9)_____. In this way she missed almost 1,000 miles (1,600 kilometers). She felt so bad about her lie that she asked for her record to be (10)_____ of the record books.

C. Match each idiom with the best definition. One definition is extra.

1. _____ as a matter of fact
2. _____ catch on
3. _____ catch one's eye
4. _____ even though
5. _____ gain an understanding
6. _____ make a comeback
7. _____ make money
8. _____ on the air
9. _____ strike it rich
10. _____ these days

a. although; despite
b. attract one's attention
c. become popular
d. become rich quickly
e. broadcast on TV or radio
f. earn money
g. have a lot of interest in something
h. in fact; actually
i. learn about; get to know something about
j. now (but not in the past)
k. return to the top level of success

D. Use the clues below to complete the crossword.

Across

1. make something useless by using it too much (2 words)
7. We've _____ toothpaste, can you please buy some at the shop? (3 words)
8. Sam wants to _____ the company after the manager retires.
9. I really want that job. I hope they _____ me.
10. decide or choose
12. make something for the first time
14. also; and (2 words)
16. a scientific idea
17. not formal; relaxed

Down

1. a large amount of money and property
2. I wanted to buy her car, but she _____ to sell it to me.
3. a writer
4. a TV station
5. cook with dry heat
6. I don't like spiders, but I'm not _____ of them.
11. guess a number or worth
12. programs and songs on TV or radio
13. a journey

14. I'm not really _____ country music.
15. *Harry Potter and the Chamber of Secrets* is a great _____.

The Puffer Fish

Before You Read

Answer the following questions.

1. What's the most unusual meal you've ever eaten?

   _____

   _____

2. What is the most expensive meal you've ever eaten?

   _____

   _____

3. What do you think is special about the fish pictured on the left?

   _____

   _____

Target Vocabulary

Match each word with the best meaning.

1. _____ breathe
2. _____ export
3. _____ identify
4. _____ import
5. _____ license
6. _____ poison
7. _____ remove
8. _____ symptom

a. something that hurts or kills people if they eat or touch it
b. take air into and out of the body
c. bring things into a country
d. send things out of a country
e. a sign of a sickness or disease
f. permission given to someone who has passed an exam
g. show or find out who someone is or what something is
h. take away

In 1996, three men in California were taken to a hospital with strange **symptoms**. They felt dizzy, tired, and weak. They couldn't speak, and they had trouble **breathing**. The hospital doctors
5 thought the men had been **poisoned**, but couldn't work out what was wrong with them. Then they found out the three men were all chefs, and they had just shared a dish of *fugu*.

Fugu, the Japanese name for the puffer fish, is
10 one of the strangest fish in the ocean. The puffer fish gets its name from the way the fish protects itself from enemies. Whenever it is attacked, the fish puffs up (blows up) its body to over twice its normal size!

15 The reason the three men were taken to the hospital is because the puffer fish is also very poisonous. As a rule, if you eat a whole puffer fish, you will probably die. The three men had a close call, but they all survived.

The symptoms of fugu poisoning are a strange feeling around the mouth and throat, and difficulty breathing. You can't breathe and your body can't get any
20 air. Your brain still works perfectly, however, so you know you are dying, but you can't speak or do anything about it.

Despite the danger of fugu poisoning, this strange, ugly, and very poisonous fish is actually a very expensive, and very popular, kind of food in Japan. Customers pay up to $200 per person to eat a fugu meal. Because of the danger, fugu can
25 only be prepared by chefs with a special **license** from the government. These chefs are trained to **identify** and **remove** the poisonous parts of the fish. Most people who die from eating fugu these days are people who have tried their hand at preparing the fish themselves.

Fugu is said to be so delicious that it has even started to be **imported** into
30 Hong Kong and the United States. Several tons of fugu are now **exported** from Japan every year.

 _____ **minutes** _____ **seconds** (331 words)

Did You Know?

The characters that make up the word "fugu" in Japanese mean "river pig," because people used to think that the puffer fish looked like a pig.

Reading Comprehension

Circle the letter of the best answer.

1. What is the best title for this passage?

    a. Fishing in Japan   **c.** The History of Fugu

    b. A Dangerous Dish   **d.** A Talented Chef

2. Why were the three men taken to the hospital?

    a. Someone poisoned them.   **c.** They poisoned each other.

    b. They ate poison by accident.   **d.** A doctor worked out their symptoms.

3. What does the puffer fish do when an enemy tries to eat it?

    a. It eats the enemy.   **c.** It looks very ugly.

    b. It makes poison.   **d.** It becomes bigger.

4. What is NOT a symptom of fugu poisoning?

    a. breathing difficulty   **c.** trouble speaking

    b. tiredness and weakness   **d.** your brain stops working

5. Who is allowed to serve fugu?

    a. people from California   **c.** the government

    b. licensed chefs   **d.** anyone who wants to try their hand

Idioms

Find each idiom in the story.

1. **as a rule**—*usually*
   - **As a rule**, it's cheaper to travel by train than fly.
   - **As a rule**, I don't drink coffee before I go to bed.

2. **try one's hand at something**—*attempt something for the first time*
   - On my vacation, I **tried my hand** at scuba diving.
   - I'd never baked a cake before, so I thought I'd **try my hand** at it.

3. **a close call**—*an accident, or death, nearly happened*
   - I had **a close call** when my car crashed.
   - The thief had **a close call** when the police almost caught him.

Vocabulary Reinforcement

A. Circle the letter of the word or phrase that best completes the sentence.

1. The United States _____ most of the oil it uses from the Middle East.
   a. exports   **b.** imports   **c.** removes   **d.** breathes

2. One of the _____ of a cold is often a high temperature.
   a. licenses   **b.** theories   **c.** poisons   **d.** symptoms

3. Australia _____ a lot of beef to countries in Asia.
   a. exports   **b.** imports   **c.** licenses   **d.** hires

4. Before they can go into that building, people must _____ themselves.
   a. prove   **b.** poison   **c.** import   **d.** identify

5. A tree fell over in my garden, so I called someone to _____ it.
   a. identify   **b.** create   **c.** remove   **d.** roast

6. Kristie had _____ when her boat sank.
   a. a close call   **b.** a journalist   **c.** as a rule   **d.** a victory

B. Complete the passage with items from the box. One item is extra.

breathe   try their hand at   license   identify   poison   symptoms

The puffer fish has a natural (1)_____ in its body. When people eat fugu that hasn't been prepared carefully, they show several strange (2)_____. The person's mouth and throat feel funny, they can't (3)_____, and they can't move. As a rule, people should not (4)_____ serving this food at home. People should only eat fugu if it is served by a chef with a special (5)_____.

What Do You Think?

1. What is a special food from your country? What food from your country would visitors from another country enjoy?

2. Would you eat fugu? What other dangerous activities would you try?

Getting Married 7

Answer the following questions.

1. Have you ever been to a wedding? Whose was it? What was it like?

   _____

   _____

2. What are some wedding traditions in your country?

   _____

   _____

3. Do you know of any famous or expensive weddings?

   _____

   _____

Target Vocabulary

Match each word with the best meaning.

1. _____ argue
2. _____ arrange
3. _____ bride
4. _____ ceremony
5. _____ complicated
6. _____ groom
7. _____ stadium
8. _____ vary

a. a formal event

b. difficult and not simple

c. fight with words

d. make plans

e. be different; change

f. a woman who is getting married

g. a man who is getting married

h. a sports playing area with seats around it

Every culture in the world has marriage and wedding **ceremonies**. Usually marriages are between one woman (the **bride**) and one man (the **groom**). However, in other parts of the world a man may have several wives, or, as in some areas of Tibet and India, a wife may have more than one husband.

5　There are also many different kinds of wedding ceremonies practiced around the world. These ceremonies can be very short and simple, or very long and **complicated**.

One of the largest and most expensive
10　wedding ceremonies in recent times was held in Dubai in 1981. The couple tying the knot at this wedding were the son of Sheik[1] Rashid Bin Saeed Al Maktoum and Princess Salama. The wedding ceremony took seven
15　days and cost $44 million. It was held in a large building which was specially built for the ceremony and looked like a **stadium**. The bride and groom needed a large place for their wedding because more than 20,000 guests were invited.

The reasons why a man and woman get married also **vary**. Sometimes they marry
20　because they are in love, sometimes they marry someone they meet through a matchmaker,[2] and sometimes they marry because their parents tell them that they must marry.

One unusual example of an **arranged** marriage took place in Bangladesh in 1986. The groom was an eleven-month-old boy and the bride was a three-month-old
25　girl. They were the youngest married couple ever.

The parents of the bride and groom arranged the marriage as a way of ending a fight between the two families who had been **arguing** over a farm for twenty years. Both families thought that they owned the farm, but no one knew exactly. The fight ended for good when the young boy married the young girl. By
30　arranging this marriage, neither family was forced to lose face. The two families agreed to give the farm to the young couple.

 _____ **minutes** _____ **seconds** (320 words)

Did You Know?

In 1921, an American couple, Joe and Annie Henry, got married. They were still married eighty years later, making them the world's longest-married couple. They have over a hundred children, grandchildren, and great-grandchildren.

[1] **Sheik** a male Arab ruler
[2] **matchmaker** a person who introduces single men and women to each other

Reading Comprehension

Circle the letter of the best answer.

1. What is the best title for this passage?

   a. An Unusual Wedding Tradition

   b. A Short History of Marriage

   c. Common Western Wedding Traditions

   d. Interesting Weddings Around the World

2. Who got married in the large wedding ceremony described in the passage?

   a. a farmer and a neighbor

   b. a king and a queen

   c. the son of a sheik and a princess

   d. two babies

3. Why was the wedding ceremony in Dubai held in a building like a stadium?

   a. The ceremony was very long.

   b. The groom loved to play sports.

   c. Many people came to the wedding.

   d. People in Dubai usually get married in stadiums.

4. Why did the families in Bangladesh make their children get married?

   a. The children were in love.

   b. The families wanted to end a fight.

   c. The families wanted to buy a farm.

   d. The bride's family wanted to sell their farm.

5. What was strange about the wedding in Bangladesh?

   a. The bride and groom were young.

   b. It was an arranged marriage.

   c. The wedding was on a farm.

   d. More than 20,000 guests came to the wedding.

Idioms

Find each idiom in the story.

1. **tie the knot**—*get married*
   - My uncle finally **tied the knot** last year.
   - We've decided to wait for a while before we **tie the knot**.

2. **lose face**—*have other people laugh at you and respect you less*
   - He thinks he'll **lose face** if he says sorry.
   - The company **lost face** when the manager was put in prison.

3. **for good**—*forever; always*
   - After years of trying, she's finally quit smoking **for good**.
   - Jackie married a Canadian man and moved to Canada **for good**.

Vocabulary Reinforcement

A. Circle the letter of the word or phrase that best completes the sentence.

1. In her white dress, Mary was a lovely _____.

   a. bride   **b.** couple   **c.** groom   **d.** parent

2. The amount of rain _____ every year. Some years are dry, others are wet.

   a. identifies   **b.** breathes   **c.** hires   **d.** varies

3. Lisa heard her neighbors _____ in the apartment next door.

   a. identifying   **b.** arguing   **c.** varying   **d.** removing

4. This machine is very _____ to use.

   a. eventually   **b.** for good   **c.** complicated   **d.** afraid

5. We _____ to meet at the theater at seven o'clock.

   a. arranged   **b.** complicated   **c.** imported   **d.** licensed

6. All the fans cheered when the team entered the _____.

   a. farm   **b.** groom   **c.** stadium   **d.** location

B. Complete the passage with items from the box. One item is extra.

arguing	for good	ceremonies	arranging	invited	groom

Some wedding (1)_____ are small, and others are very large. The largest one was held in a building that looked like a stadium, and 20,000 guests were (2)_____! Another interesting wedding was between a bride and (3)_____ who were babies from two families who had been (4)_____ over some land. This wedding ended the fight (5)_____.

What Do You Think?

1. What is the average age to get married in your country? What do you think is the best age to get married?

2. If you were getting married, what kind of wedding would you have? Where would you hold it? Who would you invite?

Say It with Flowers

Before You Read

Answer the following questions.

1. Have you ever given flowers to someone as a gift? If yes, who?

_____

_____

2. What kind of flowers do you like to give or receive? Why?

_____

_____

3. Do different flowers have different meanings in your country?

_____

_____

Target Vocabulary

Match each word with the best meaning.

1. _____ basket

2. _____ bunch

3. _____ custom

4. _____ decrease

5. _____ feather

6. _____ pure

7. _____ remain

8. _____ wax

a. tradition; a way to do things from the past

b. stay; continue

c. one of the things that cover a bird

d. the material a candle is made from

e. a group of many things

f. clean; without dirt or pollution

g. make or become less or smaller

h. an open container used for carrying things, usually made from plant material

These days it is very common for young men to give flowers to young women when they are in love, but this hasn't always been the **custom**.

In the 1700s in Turkey, it was quite popular for people in love to secretly send each other **baskets** full of strange things. Usually, an old woman who sold flowers
5 or fruit on the street left the basket beside the door of the person receiving it.

These gift baskets included a variety of objects, such as flowers, stones, **feathers**, **wax**, and even charcoal.[1] Each thing in the basket had a special
10 meaning and by figuring out the secret message contained in each item, the person who received the basket could determine the true feelings of the giver.

This idea of sending gifts of love with
15 secret meanings quickly spread to Germany, France, and England. However, over time, only sending flowers **remained** popular.

A **bunch** of flowers told young ladies about the feelings in the hearts of young
20 men. Each different flower had a different meaning. For example, the flowers from an orange tree meant, "You are beautiful and **pure**." Pink carnations meant, "My love for you is strong and great." Yellow roses, on the other hand, meant, "I saw you with someone else."

Many flower dictionaries were made to help young people in love understand the
25 meaning of the flowers they received. Not all of the dictionaries agreed, however, on the meaning of each flower, so a person had to watch out what flowers they chose to send. For example, depending on which dictionary you used, and which color you gave, a young man's roses could mean, "I love you," "love is dangerous," or even, "my love has **decreased**."

30 By the 1880s, using flowers to send messages had fallen out of fashion, and the more direct way of sending love letters began. Today, flowers are still considered a lovely gift, but the meaning for each kind of flower has been lost.

_____ **minutes** _____ **seconds** (328 words)

> ### Did You Know?
> Americans spend almost $15 billion a year on flowers. The most popular flower is the rose, of which there are more than 2,000 different varieties.

[1] **charcoal** a black material made by burning wood

Reading Comprehension

Circle the letter of the best answer.

1. What custom is described in the second and third paragraphs?

    a. sending gift baskets

    b. selling gift baskets

    c. sending flowers

    d. selling flowers

2. What did the items in a gift basket explain to the receiver?

    a. the receiver's looks

    b. the sender's feelings

    c. the receiver's personality

    d. the sender's name

3. To where did the idea of sending gifts of love spread?

    a. Asia

    b. Europe

    c. Turkey

    d. North America

4. How did people know the meaning of each kind of flower?

    a. They found out from books.

    b. Old women explained it.

    c. The sender told them.

    d. They read secret letters.

5. In which century did the custom of reading messages through flowers become uncommon?

    a. the seventeenth century

    b. the eighteenth century

    c. the nineteenth century

    d. the twentieth century

Idioms

Find each idiom in the story.

1. **fall out of fashion**—*lose popularity*
    - For men, wearing hats has **fallen out of fashion**.
    - As people write more e-mails, letter-writing has really **fallen out of fashion**.

2. **watch out (for)**—*be careful*
    - **Watch out!** That car's going to hit us!
    - **Watch out for** snakes when you're walking in the woods.

3. **on the other hand**—*however (used to introduce an opposite idea)*
    - A lot of people don't like washing dishes. I, **on the other hand**, really enjoy it.
    - Big dogs can be expensive to keep. **On the other hand**, they are great pets.

Vocabulary Reinforcement

A. Circle the letter of the word or phrase that means the same as the words in *italics*.

1. The number of people in this country *decreases* every year.

   a. goes up   **b.** goes down   **c.** stays the same   **d.** varies

2. I love chocolate. *On the other hand,* my wife hates it.

   a. as a matter of fact   **b.** in fact   **c.** however   **d.** as a rule

3. The water in this river is not *clean.* Do not drink it.

   a. pure   **b.** wax   **c.** feather   **d.** complicated

4. You should *watch out for* bears in these woods.

   a. go away from   **b.** be careful of   **c.** discover   **d.** refuse

5. It is a *tradition* to eat cake on your birthday.

   a. basket   **b.** wax   **c.** gift   **d.** custom

6. It's difficult for Robert to explain his *feelings.*

   a. emotions   **b.** secrets   **c.** information   **d.** fashion

B. Complete the passage with items from the box. One item is extra.

> fell out of fashion   bunch   basket   remains   decreases   custom

In Turkey, people used to follow the (1)_____ of sending special things to people they loved. A man would send a (2)_____ full of things to a woman. Each thing had a special meaning. After the custom spread to Europe, people would send a (3)_____ of flowers with special meanings. Later, the meanings (4)_____, but giving flowers to someone you love (5)_____ popular today.

What Do You Think?

1. When do people give flowers in your country? Do different flowers have different meanings?

2. If you were going to give a gift basket to someone, what would you put in it? Would the things in it have special meanings?

Bollywood

Bollywood director Ashutosh Gowariker

Before You Read

Answer the following questions.

1. What do you know about Hollywood?

2. Have you seen any films that weren't made in the United States or in your country?

3. What other countries are famous for their movies?

Target Vocabulary

Match each word with the best meaning.

1. _____ adventure   **a.** all businesses that make or sell a product

2. _____ compare   **b.** see how two things are the same or different

3. _____ costume   **c.** clothes worn by an actor or actress

4. _____ industry   **d.** in a film, the background behind an actor or actress

5. _____ mystery   **e.** the words that the actors in a film say

6. _____ scenery   **f.** something that's difficult to explain

7. _____ script   **g.** an exciting or dangerous journey

8. _____ shoot (a film) **h.** take pictures with a movie camera

Most people think that the capital of the movie world is Hollywood, in the United States. However, the real movie capital is Mumbai, in India. Mumbai used to be known
5   as Bombay, and so the film[1] **industry** there is called "Bollywood." Bollywood makes twice as many movies each year as Hollywood— more than 800 films a year.

The movies from Bollywood are very
10 different from Hollywood movies. For one thing, Bollywood movies are much longer than most Hollywood movies. Most Bollywood movies are more than three hours long, and contain singing, dancing, action,
15 **adventure**, **mystery**, and romance (but usually

Bollywood actress Aishwarya Rai

no kissing). Because Bollywood films contain so many different features, this style of film is sometimes called a "masala" film. ("Masala" is an Indian word for a mixture of spices.[2])

Another big difference between Bollywood and Hollywood movies is the way the
20 movies are made. It takes much longer to make a movie in Hollywood than in Bollywood. In fact, filming may begin on a Bollywood movie before the **script** is even finished. The director and writers can make up the story while the film is being made. Sometimes they will even write the script by hand instead of taking time to type it.

25 Bollywood actors are very popular and some are in such high demand that they may work on several movies at the same time. They may even **shoot** scenes for several films on the same day using the same **costumes** and **scenery**. Since most Bollywood movies follow the same kind of story, shooting scenes for several films at the same time is not a big problem for actors or directors. This also helps keep
30 the cost of Bollywood movies lower than the cost of Hollywood movies. The average Bollywood film, with a budget of only two million U.S. dollars, seems very cheap **compared** to the average budget of sixty million U.S. dollars for a Hollywood film—thirty times as much!

 _____ **minutes** _____ **seconds** (323 words)

Did You Know?

A hundred million people go to the cinema every week in India.

---

[1] **film** movie
[2] **spices** part of a plant, or powder from part of a plant, that you put in food to make it tasty, e.g., pepper, ginger, curry powder, cardamom

Reading Comprehension

Circle the letter of the best answer.

1. What is the main topic of the reading?

    a. famous stars in Bollywood

    b. how Hollywood movies are made

    c. the differences between two movie industries

    d. the history of movie-making in India

2. What is NOT true about Mumbai?

    a. It is the movie capital of India.

    b. The new name is Bombay.

    c. More movies are made there than in Hollywood.

    d. It is less expensive to make films there than in Hollywood.

3. Why are Bollywood films often called "masala" films?

    a. They have spicy stories.

    b. They show Indian culture.

    c. They are much longer than Hollywood films.

    d. They mix different styles of movies.

4. Bollywood movies are cheap to make because . . .

    a. they are shorter than Hollywood films.

    b. the scripts are written by hand.

    c. the movies do not use any special effects.

    d. each movie reuses things from other movies.

5. Which of these statements would the writer probably agree with?

    a. Hollywood movies are too violent.

    b. It takes a lot of money to make a good movie.

    c. Only Indian people can understand Bollywood movies.

    d. Most Bollywood movies are very similar.

Idioms

Find each idiom in the story.

1. **in (high) demand**—*wanted by or popular with many people*
    - The book was **in high demand**, and the bookstores sold out very quickly.
    - There's only one doctor in that town, so she's always **in demand**.

2. **by hand**—*without using machines*
    - I can type much faster than I can write **by hand**.
    - The rugs were very expensive because each one was made **by hand**.

3. **for one thing**—*as one example*
    - I don't like him. **For one thing**, he's always late.
    - I know this isn't my dog. **For one thing**, my dog is much smaller.

Vocabulary Reinforcement

A. Circle the letter of the word or phrase that best completes the sentence.

1. The director wants to _____ his new adventure movie in the jungle.
   a. arrange   **b.** contain   **c.** shoot   **d.** create

2. The writer changed the movie's _____ five times.
   a. article   **b.** material   **c.** novel   **d.** script

3. The photocopier was broken, so she copied the class notes _____.
   a. by hand   **b.** for good   **c.** on the other hand   **d.** in high demand

4. If you _____ these two watches carefully, you can tell which is best.
   a. license   **b.** compare   **c.** arrange   **d.** decrease

5. People in the movie _____ can earn a lot of money.
   a. scenery   **b.** costume   **c.** industry   **d.** mystery

6. No one knew the movie was shot in a studio, because the _____ looked so real.
   a. scenery   **b.** script   **c.** costumes   **d.** feathers

B. Complete the passage with items from the box. One item is extra.

shoot   for one thing   industry   adventures   costumes   compare

Bollywood is the name of the movie (1)_____ in India. Film-makers in Bollywood actually (2)_____ twice as many movies each year as film-makers in Hollywood. If you (3)_____ the movies of the two industries, you can see several differences. (4)_____, Bollywood movies are much longer than the average Hollywood movie. In addition, Bollywood movies reuse scenery and (5)_____ to keep the cost of the films low.

What Do You Think?

1. Why do you think that Bollywood films are not as successful in other countries as Hollywood films?

2. If you could make a movie, what would it be about, and who would star in it?

The Nobel Prize 10

Nobel Prize winners Nelson Mandela (center) and F. W. de Klerk (right)

Before You Read

Answer the following questions.

1. What famous international prizes do you know? _____

2. What do you know about the Nobel Prize? _____

3. Do you know any Nobel Prize winners? _____

Target Vocabulary

Match each word with the best meaning.

1. _____ aim
2. _____ announcement
3. _____ annual
4. _____ category
5. _____ explosive
6. _____ (to) found (something)
7. _____ individual
8. _____ interest

a. one person

b. start a building or organization

c. happening every year

d. a group or type of thing

e. a percentage paid on an amount of money

f. a material used to blow up things

g. something that is made public, or said to many people

h. purpose; goal

43

Each year on December 10, the world's attention turns to Sweden for the **announcement** of the Nobel Prize winners. The Nobel Prizes, six prizes given to groups or **individuals** who really stand out in their fields,[1] were **founded** by a Swedish inventor, Alfred Nobel.

5 Alfred Nobel was the man who invented dynamite, a powerful **explosive**. During his life, Nobel made a lot of money from his invention, and he decided that he wanted to use his money to help scientists, artists, and people who worked to help others around the world. When he died, his will[2] said that the money would be placed in a bank, and the **interest** the money earned would be given out as five
10 **annual** cash prizes.

The prizes set up by Nobel were first handed out in 1901, and include physics, medicine, chemistry, literature, and peace. Later, in 1968 the Bank of Sweden added a prize in economics to celebrate the bank's 300th year of business.

Each person who receives a Nobel Prize is
15 given a cash prize, a medal, and a certificate. The prize money for each **category** is currently worth about a million dollars, and the **aim** of the prize is to allow the winner to carry on working or researching without
20 having to worry about raising money.

The prizes can be given to either individuals or groups. Prize winners include Albert Einstein (physics, 1921), Kenzaburo Oe (literature, 1994), Kim Dae Jung (peace,
25 2001), the United Nations (peace, 2001), and Nelson Mandela (peace, 1993).

Nobel Prize winner Kim Dae Jung (right)

The prize winner that has won the most times is the International Committee of the Red Cross. This organization has received three Nobel Peace Prizes (in 1917,
30 1944, and 1963), and the founder, Jean Henri Dunant, was awarded the first Nobel Peace Prize, in 1901.

_____ **minutes** _____ **seconds** (296 words)

Did You Know?

Marie Curie was the first woman to win a Nobel Prize. She first won for physics in 1903, and she then won again in 1911 for chemistry. Her husband, daughter, and son-in-law were also all Nobel Prize winners.

---

[1] **field** an area of study or interest; a specialty
[2] **will** a letter saying who will inherit your money and property after you die

Reading Comprehension

Circle the letter of the best answer.

1. What is the best title for this passage?

   a. The History of the Nobel Prize

   b. The Nobel Peace Prize

   c. How to Win a Nobel Prize

   d. Famous International Prizes

2. How many categories of Nobel Prize did Alfred Nobel found?

   a. one

   b. five

   c. six

   d. The article doesn't say.

3. How did Alfred Nobel become rich?

   a. by winning a Nobel Prize

   b. through his inventions

   c. through the interest on his savings

   d. by receiving money from the Bank of Sweden

4. What statement about the Nobel Prizes is NOT true?

   a. They are given out every year.

   b. They can't be given to the same winner more than once.

   c. They are worth about a million dollars each.

   d. They are given to both individuals and groups.

5. Who or what was the first Nobel Peace Prize Winner?

   a. Alfred Nobel

   b. Albert Einstein

   c. Jean Henri Dunant

   d. the International Committee of the Red Cross

Idioms

Find each idiom in the story.

1. **set up**—*found; start*
   - The bank teller helped me **set up** my new bank account.
   - Wendy needed to ask for help in **setting up** her new computer.

2. **carry on**—*continue*
   - Sorry for disturbing you. **Carry on** with what you were doing.
   - Frank was so tired that it was difficult for him to **carry on**.

3. **hand out**—*give to many people*
   - The teacher **handed out** the notes at the beginning of class.
   - Jenny's part-time job is **handing out** advertising flyers on the street.

Vocabulary Reinforcement

A. Circle the letter of the word or phrase that best completes the sentence.

1. The students _____ talking, even though their teacher was waiting for silence.
   a. ruled out   **b.** wore out   **c.** carried on   **d.** handed out

2. At the airport, Harvey listened for the _____ to tell him when his plane was leaving.
   a. announcement   **b.** explosive   **c.** category   **d.** script

3. Every August I go to the town's _____ festival.
   a. complicated   **b.** individual   **c.** annual   **d.** estimated

4. On the wall of the bank there is a portrait of the man who _____ it.
   a. announced   **b.** remained   **c.** poisoned   **d.** founded

5. Groups of people usually take longer to make a decision than _____.
   a. individuals   **b.** costumes   **c.** baskets   **d.** categories

6. At the party it was difficult to tell people apart because everyone was wearing _____.
   a. a category   **b.** a costume   **c.** a feather   **d.** an announcement

B. Complete the passage with items from the box. One item is extra.

aim	set up	categories	interest	explosive	hand out

The Nobel Prizes are awards (1)_____ by Alfred Nobel. This inventor got rich from making dynamite, an (2)_____. Some of Nobel's money is still in the bank, and (3)_____ from this money is given to the winners of the Nobel Prizes. The (4)_____ of the prizes is to allow people to work or research without worrying about money. There are six (5)_____ of prizes: physics, medicine, chemistry, literature, peace, and economics.

What Do You Think?

1. Can you think of a person who should win a Nobel Prize? Which award should they receive, and for what reason(s)?

2. If you wanted to win a Nobel Prize, what would you do?

Review

A. Find words for each definition. Two words are extra.

compare	complicated	costume	decrease	explosive
groom	import	interest	poison	remain	remove	symptom

1. _____ something that hurts or kills people if they eat or touch it
2. _____ make or become less or smaller
3. _____ bring things into a country
4. _____ see how two things are the same or different
5. _____ a sign of a sickness or disease
6. _____ clothes worn by an actor or actress
7. _____ difficult; not simple
8. _____ a percentage paid on an amount of money
9. _____ a man who is getting married
10. _____ a material used to blow up things

B. Complete the paragraph with items from the box. Two items are extra.

annual	aimed	announcements	as a rule	categories	compared
founded	handed out	identified	industry	individuals	on the other hand

For American journalists, photographers, and authors, the most important (1)_____
awards are not the Nobel Prize, but the Pulitzer Prizes. The Pulitzer Prizes were
(2)_____ by Joseph Pulitzer, an American journalist, in 1904, and were divided into
eleven (3)_____, including journalism, nonfiction books, and novels. In the years since
then the number of prizes that are (4)_____ has increased to twenty-one, but
(5)_____ they are still mainly (6)_____ at newspaper journalists—both
(7)_____ and groups.

For people working in the American newspaper (8)_____, the day in April when the
prize (9)_____ are made, and winners are (10)_____, is one of the most
important of the year.

C. Match each idiom with the best definition. One definition is extra.

1. _____ a close call
2. _____ by hand
3. _____ carry on
4. _____ for good
5. _____ for one thing
6. _____ in demand
7. _____ on the other hand
8. _____ tie the knot
9. _____ try one's hand at something
10. _____ watch out for

a. be careful
b. however
c. wanted by or popular with many people
d. death or an accident nearly happened
e. forever; always
f. attempt something for the first time
g. as an example
h. lose popularity
i. continue
j. marry
k. without using machines

D. Use the clues below to complete the crossword.

Across

5. He gave her a beautiful _____ of flowers.
7. It was a beautiful wedding _____.
8. a sports playing area with seats around it
10. Don't _____ with me! Just do what I tell you!
11. one of the things that a bird is covered with
14. what candles are made from
15. The water from this river is so _____ you can drink it.
18. in a film, the background behind the actors
19. People die if they spend too long underwater and can't _____.

Down

1. I can't wait until I'm eighteen and I can get my driver's _____.
2. Megan is afraid to make mistakes because she thinks she will _____. (2 words)
3. take pictures with a movie camera
4. be different; change
6. the words that an actor reads
9. Giving chocolate on St. Valentine's Day is a quite recent _____.
10. make plans
12. an exciting or dangerous journey
13. Saudi Arabia _____ a lot of oil to other countries.

16. a small open container used for carrying things
17. Thanks for helping me _____ my new computer. (2 words)

A Funny Cure

Before You Read

Answer the following questions.

1. What do you usually do when you have a cold?

_____

_____

2. What kinds of illnesses do you think can be cured without going to a doctor?

_____

_____

3. Look at the title of this unit. What do you think the reading is about?

_____

_____

Target Vocabulary

Match each word with the best meaning.

1. _____ amusing

2. _____ cure

3. _____ disease

4. _____ editor

5. _____ experiment

6. _____ health

7. _____ issue

8. _____ painful

a. well being; condition of the body

b. a topic or subject that people are concerned about

c. a sickness or serious illness

d. funny

e. hurting

f. (noun) a scientific test; (verb) test scientifically

g. medicine or treatment that makes a sick person healthy again

h. a person in charge of publishing a book, magazine, or newspaper

An old English saying[1] says, "Laughter is the best medicine." One person who certainly would have agreed with this is Norman Cousins.

Norman Cousins was the **editor** of a magazine
5   called Saturday Review for almost forty years. He also wrote and spoke about world peace and anti-nuclear and anti-war[2] **issues**, traveling to many different countries to share his ideas.

In the 1960s, after returning to the United States
10   from a busy and tiring trip to Europe, Mr. Cousins got sick. He discovered he had a rare **disease**, known as *ankylosing spondylitis*, that caused the joints[3] between his bones to become stiff.

In less than a week after he got back, he could not stand. Every move that he
15   made was **painful**. He was not able to sleep at night. The doctors told Mr. Cousins that they did not know how to **cure** his problem and he might never get over the illness. Mr. Cousins, however, refused to give up hope.

Mr. Cousins thought that the illness could be caused by unhappy thoughts. He did not want to take medicine to cure himself. Instead, he felt that happy
20   thoughts or laughter might cure his illness.

He began to **experiment** on himself while still in the hospital by watching comedy shows on television. Mr. Cousins quickly found that ten minutes of real laughter during the day gave him two hours of pain-free[4] sleep at night.

Deciding that the doctors could not help him, Mr. Cousins left the hospital and
25   checked into a hotel room where he could continue his experiments with laughter. For eight days, Mr. Cousins rested in the hotel room watching comedy shows on television, reading **amusing** books, and sleeping whenever he felt tired. Within three weeks, he felt well enough to take a vacation to Puerto Rico where he began running on the beach for exercise.

30   After a few months, Mr. Cousins was able to carry on his work. He had laughed himself back to **health**.

_____ **minutes** _____ **seconds** (327 words)

Did You Know?
According to studies, young children laugh 400 times a day, while adults laugh only 15 times a day.

[1] **saying** a clever thought that many people know and say, such as a proverb
[2] **anti-nuclear, anti-war** the prefix "anti-" means you disagree with the thing; nuclear refers to nuclear weapons
[3] **joints** the areas between bones that can bend, e.g., knees and elbows
[4] **pain-free** the suffix "-free" means "without"; pain-free means "without pain"

Reading Comprehension

Circle the letter of the best answer.

1. What is the main topic of the reading?

   a. a funny story

   b. an interesting cure

   c. an amazing life

   d. why people laugh

2. What is NOT true about *ankylosing spondylitis*?

   a. It is uncommon.

   b. It makes walking difficult.

   c. It is easily cured.

   d. It is painful.

3. What did the doctors think about Mr. Cousin's disease?

   a. It could be cured if he slept more.

   b. It might never be cured.

   c. It could be cured by taking medicine.

   d. It would take a week to get over it.

4. What did Mr. Cousins think cured him?

   a. laughter

   b. running on the beach

   c. medicine

   d. taking a vacation

5. What did Mr. Cousins do after he got better?

   a. He went back to the hospital.

   b. He continued his job.

   c. He wrote amusing books.

   d. The passage doesn't say.

Idioms

Find each idiom in the story.

1. **get back**—*return*
   - Give me a call when you **get back** from your vacation.
   - I've got a lot of work to do when I **get back** to the office.

2. **get over**—*get better after a sickness*
   - I feel terrible. I hope I **get over** this cold soon.
   - It took Fiona a long time to **get over** her illness.

3. **check in(to)/out (of)**—*enter/leave a hotel*
   - **Check in** time at that hotel is from 4 P.M.
   - I had an early morning flight, so I **checked into** the airport hotel.

Vocabulary Reinforcement

A. Circle the letter of the word or phrase that best completes the sentence.

1. Doug never exercises. I'm worried about his _____.
   a. cure   **b.** issue   **c.** health   **d.** experiment

2. Jo works as an _____ for a publishing company.
   a. article   **b.** editor   **c.** experiment   **d.** explorer

3. Paul's really interested in _____ like saving nature.
   a. issues   **b.** diseases   **c.** experiments   **d.** ceremonies

4. I'm looking forward to _____ the hotel and having a shower.
   a. getting over   **b.** checking into   **c.** setting up   **d.** watching out for

5. The train arrives at ten, so I'll probably _____ the office at 10:30.
   a. check out of   **b.** set up   **c.** get back to   **d.** catch the eye of

6. Patricia's a funny woman. She always tells _____ stories.
   a. amusing   **b.** painful   **c.** pure   **d.** casual

B. Complete the passage with items from the box. One item is extra.

get over   painful   cure   issue   experiment   disease

Norman Cousins had a very strange (1)_____ which made his joints stiff, and it was (2)_____ for him to move around. Doctors could not (3)_____ his illness, and they said he may never (4)_____ it. But Mr. Cousins started to (5)_____ with laughter and he was finally able to get back to work.

What Do You Think?

1. What makes you laugh?
2. Who are the funniest people in your country? How about in the world?

Palm Reading

Before You Read

Answer the following questions.

1. Has anyone ever told your fortune?
   If yes, how did they do it?

2. Do you believe it is possible to tell someone's
   fortune by using the lines on their hand?

3. Some people think the lines on your palm have different
   meanings. Do you know what these meanings are?

Target Vocabulary

Match each word with the best meaning.

1. _____ fate   **a.** the inside part of the hand with lines on it

2. _____ imagination   **b.** big; important

3. _____ leadership   **c.** small; less important

4. _____ major   **d.** a power that decides a person's future

5. _____ minor   **e.** a connection between ideas, people, or things

6. _____ palm   **f.** ability to lead people

7. _____ relationship   **g.** creativity; creating stories or pictures in the mind

8. _____ represent   **h.** show; mean; stand for; replace

Even for people who don't believe in fortune telling, it can be fun to learn about what fortune-tellers look at on a person's **palm**.

To read a person's future, a fortune-teller looks at both of the person's hands. The hand that a person uses for writing will show the things the person has done in
5 life, and the choices he or she has made. The person's other hand will show the abilities they were born with, and their fate.

In palm reading, most people know that different lines on the hand **represent** things about a person's life. For example, there are three **major** lines on everyone's hands called the head line, heart line, and life line.

10 The head line represents intelligence—people with a long head line are said to have an excellent memory, while those with a short one are very intelligent. The life line represents health, and the longer it is, the healthier someone is. The heart line represents emotions and **relationships**—as a rule, the longer it is, the more important relationships are to that person.

15 There are also six **minor** lines, but quite a lot of people do not have one or more of the minor lines. The minor lines represent things such as the person's **fate**, wealth, health, marriage life, and children. Fortune-tellers read these lines by looking at how deep and how long each line is.

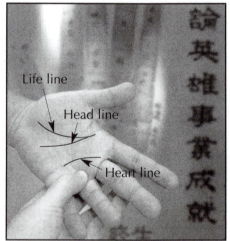

Life line
Head line
Heart line

20 In addition, fortune-tellers believe they can read information from the fingers of the hand. Each finger has a certain skill or fortune related to it. The thumb is related to love, the index finger to **leadership**, the middle finger to fate, the ring
25 finger to art and **imagination**, and the smallest finger to communication. A fortune-teller will look at the length of each finger, how the finger bends, the size of the joints, and the shape of the ends of the fingers.

_____ **minutes** _____ **seconds** (314 words)

Reading Comprehension

Circle the letter of the best answer.

1. What is the main topic of the reading?

   a. how fortune-tellers read palms   **c.** a famous fortune-teller

   b. the history of palm reading   **d.** why palm reading is popular today

2. Which is NOT important for reading palms?

   a. the depth of the lines   **c.** the size of the hand

   b. the length of the fingers   **d.** which hand is used

3. What should a fortune-teller look at to read a person's future?

   a. the back of the person's hand   **c.** the hand not used for writing

   b. the fingers of the left hand   **d.** the person's stronger hand

4. If a person has a long index finger with a good shape, which job would probably suit the person?

   a. actor   **c.** journalist

   b. manager   **d.** writer

5. What is true about the minor lines on the palm?

   a. Some people might not have all of them.

   b. Few people are interested in these lines.

   c. The lines make the meaning of the fingers stronger.

   d. They are more difficult for fortune-tellers to read.

Idioms

Find each idiom in the story.

1. **believe in**—*think that something is true or a good idea*
   - I don't **believe in** ghosts or witches.
   - He **believed in** helping people, so he worked as a doctor in Africa.

2. **be related to**—*have a connection to*
   - She said she is **related to** the Russian royal family.
   - This paragraph is not **related to** the rest of the article.

3. **quite a lot (of)**—*many; much; quite a few*
   - I studied **quite a lot** for the test, but I am still nervous.
   - He has **quite a lot of** money in the bank.

Vocabulary Reinforcement

A. Circle the letter of the word or phrase that best completes the sentence.

1. She strongly _____ giving money to her church.
   a. believes in   **b.** is related to   **c.** hands out   **d.** represents

2. I am always surprised by the _____ of great painters.
   a. thumbs   **b.** health   **c.** imagination   **d.** symptoms

3. The color white on the flag _____ the country's belief in peace and freedom.
   a. founds   **b.** decreases   **c.** argues   **d.** represents

4. It was their _____ to meet and fall in love.
   a. fate   **b.** leadership   **c.** interest   **d.** atmosphere

5. It is important for a manager to have strong _____ skills.
   a. explosive   **b.** leadership   **c.** major   **d.** complicated

6. May and her sister have a very close _____.
   a. relationship   **b.** personal   **c.** roast   **d.** compare

B. Complete the passage with items from the box. One item is extra.

health   are related to   believe in   palms   minor   fate

Some people ask fortune-tellers to read their (1)_____ in order to find out their (2)_____. Fortune-tellers look at a person's fingers and the lines on both hands. There are three major lines on the hand, and several (3)_____ ones as well. These smaller lines (4)_____ such things as a person's wealth, marriage, life, and (5)_____.

What Do You Think?

1. Look at your own, or someone else's, palm. What do the lines tell you? Do you believe it?
2. What other methods of fortune telling do you know? Do you think any of these methods can really tell the future?

Amazing Memory 13

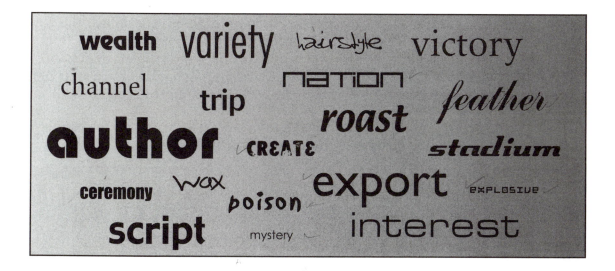

wealth   variety   hairstyle   victory

channel   trip   nation   feather

author   roast   CREATE   stadium

ceremony   wax   export   explosive

poison

script   mystery   interest

Before You Read

Answer the following questions.

1. Do you think that you have a good memory?

2. How do you usually remember things? Which do you find easiest to remember—names, faces, or numbers?

3. Look at the words in the box for one minute, then close your book. Without looking, how many of the vocabulary items can you remember?

Target Vocabulary

Match each word with the best meaning.

1. _____ associate (something with something)

2. _____ constant

3. _____ eternal

4. _____ memorize

5. _____ order

6. _____ random

7. _____ runner-up

8. _____ unfortunately

a. remember something exactly

b. unluckily; by bad luck

c. the way things are arranged; sequence

d. connect something in the mind

e. unplanned; happening in any place or at any time

f. forever; never-ending

g. (adj.) not changing; (noun) a number that does not change

h. someone who comes second place in a race or contest

Give this memory test a try. Mix up the cards in a deck[1] of playing cards. Now look at the top seven cards for a second each. Can you remember them in order?

Contestants at the annual World Memory Championships can. In fact, the 2002 champion, Andi Bell, **memorized** the **random order** of 23 decks of cards (that's
5 1,196 cards) after looking at them for only an hour! In the same competition, Andi Bell memorized 182 random words in fifteen minutes, and a ten-year-old German girl, Lara Hick, memorized 75 faces and names in fifteen minutes.

Nine years earlier, another memorizer, Dominic O'Brien (who was the **runner-up** in the 2002 event) memorized the order of 40 decks of cards after looking at each
10 one once. He only made one mistake.

In 1987, a Japanese man, Hideaki Tomoyori, wanted to prove that his memory was the best in the world by remembering by heart *pi* (π), a **constant** number in math which starts 3.14159 . . .
15 This number never repeats itself or ends. He recited pi to 40,000 decimal places.[2] It took the fifty-five-year-old man more than twelve hours to say the numbers, but he did it without making a mistake!

To remember pi, Mr. Tomoyori divided the number
20 into groups of ten digits,[3] and **associated** each number with a sound. He then made up stories to help him remember the words he made from the sounds. In an interview after his achievement, he said, "I decided to go ahead and memorize the value of that **eternal** number pi up to one thousand places. But it wasn't easy—in fact, it took
25 me three years. To get to 40,000 decimal places it took me about ten years."

Unfortunately for Mr. Tomoyori, his record was broken in 1995, when another Japanese man, Hiroyuki Goto, memorized pi to 42,195 places.

 _____ minutes _____ seconds (308 words)

Did You Know?

Most of the champions in the World Memory Championships use a technique called "the method of loci." In this technique, objects to be remembered are placed along an imaginary pathway which the memorizer follows to remember the items in order.

---

[1] **deck** a pack of 52 playing cards
[2] **decimal places** digits to the right of the dot in a number, e.g., 6.4323 has four decimal places
[3] **digit** a single number (0 to 9)

Reading Comprehension

Circle the letter of the best answer.

1. What is the best title for this passage?

   a. Great Memory Techniques

   b. Incredible Memorizers

   c. Strange Competitions

   d. Amazing Card Tricks

2. How many cards did Dominic O'Brien memorize at the 2002 World Memory Championships?

   a. 40

   b. 1,196

   c. 2,080

   d. The passage doesn't say.

3. Why was Lara Hick's achievement special?

   a. She was female.

   b. She was German.

   c. She was young.

   d. She had the best memory in the championships.

4. What sentence is probably true about Hideaki Tomoyori?

   a. He has a good imagination.

   b. He only made one mistake.

   c. He found remembering pi quite easy.

   d. He has a better memory than Hiroyuki Goto.

5. Who remembered the greatest number of things or numbers?

   a. Dominic O'Brien

   b. Andi Bell

   c. Hideaki Tomoyori

   d. Hiroyuki Goto

Idioms

Find each idiom in the story.

1. **give (something) a try**—*attempt something for the first time*
   - I've never been scuba diving before, but I'd love to **give it a try**.
   - You should **give** snowboarding **a try**. It's a lot of fun.

2. **make up**—*invent*
   - Blake loves **making up** stories to tell his children.
   - Amanda needed to **make up** a good reason for why she was late for work.

3. **by heart**—*by memory*
   - Anne learned two hundred words **by heart** for the test.
   - Colin remembered the poem **by heart**.

Vocabulary Reinforcement

A. Circle the letter of the word or phrase that best completes the sentence.

1. Humphrey didn't win the race, but he did finish _____.
   a. eternal   **b.** decimal   **c.** order   **d.** runner-up

2. I know you aren't really into karaoke, but you should _____.
   a. give it a try   **b.** carry on   **c.** tie the knot   **d.** make up

3. Death is sometimes called "_____ sleep."
   a. random   **b.** eternal   **c.** unfortunate   **d.** for good

4. The children stood _____ from shortest to tallest.
   a. runner-up   **b.** related to   **c.** in order   **d.** associated

5. I have a lot of words to _____ for the test next week.
   a. by heart   **b.** memorize   **c.** train   **d.** associate

6. Can you _____ that strange animal?
   a. memorize   **b.** make up   **c.** found   **d.** identify

B. Complete the passage with items from the box. One item is extra.

constant	associated	eternal	made up	random	by heart

There are some people with amazing memory skills. One man memorized the order of thousands of (1)_____ cards after seeing them only one time. Another man from Japan memorized pi (2)_____. This number is a mathematical (3)_____ that never repeats. To memorize this number, the man (4)_____ groups of numbers with sounds and words. Then he (5)_____ stories with these words to remember them. He memorized pi to 40,000 places this way.

What Do You Think?

1. Do you think you can improve your memory through practice? What kind of practice do you think works best?

2. Mr. Tomoyori spent ten years to break a record. Do you think it was worth the time? What record would you like to break?

Incredible Dogs 14

Before You Read

Answer the following questions.

1. Do you have any pets?
   What kinds of pets are popular in your country? _____

2. Do you know of any animals that have
   done amazing things? _____

3. How big do you think the largest dog was?
   How about the smallest dog? _____

Target Vocabulary

Match each word with the best meaning.

1. _____ blanket
2. _____ bravery
3. _____ companion
4. _____ documentary
5. _____ recover
6. _____ remarkable
7. _____ reward
8. _____ wheelchair

a. someone that goes or lives with another person; friend
b. a warm bed covering
c. not being afraid of danger
d. get better after being sick or injured
e. incredible; amazing
f. a chair with wheels for people who can't walk
g. a television show or film based on true facts
h. (noun) a prize given for doing something good;
       (verb) to give such a prize

For thousands of years, people have lived with dogs. Ancient paintings on the walls of caves show people living with dogs. Almost a third of the homes in the United States and England have dogs, and these dogs come in a wide variety of shapes and sizes.

5 The largest dog in the world was a dog named Zorba. When Zorba, a mastiff,[1] was seven years old in 1989, he was 94 centimeters (37 inches) tall. In other words, Zorba was more than half as tall as an adult man. At his largest, Zorba weighed more than a heavyweight boxer[2] at 156 kilograms (343 pounds).

In comparison, the smallest dog was a Yorkshire 10 terrier from England. This dog was only the size of a matchbox, measuring 7.1 centimeters (2.8 inches) tall and 9.5 centimeters (3.75 inches) from nose to tail. The dog weighed about half as much as this book, and even a young child could easily 15 pick it up with one hand. It passed away in 1945 when it was only two years old.

Some dogs are **remarkable**, not for their size, but for their brain. One incredible dog is Endal, the **companion** of a man named Allen Parton who has 20 used a **wheelchair** since a car accident in 1991.

In 2001, Parton was hit by a car while crossing a road with Endal, and thrown out of his chair. Endal quickly moved Parton into the **recovery** position,[3] covered him with a **blanket**, and pushed his mobile phone close enough 25 for him to reach. Then, once he saw that Parton was all right, Endal ran back and forth to a nearby hotel, barking until people came out to help.

Endal was **rewarded** for his **bravery** by being awarded a medal, and he has been the subject of a number of TV **documentaries**.

_____ **minutes** _____ **seconds** (302 words)

Did You Know?

The photo of the dog on this page is the actual size of the world's smallest dog!

---

[1] **mastiff** a large dog often used as a guard dog
[2] **boxer** a person who fights with his fists, usually for money
[3] **recovery position** a way of placing unconscious people so they are safe

Reading Comprehension

Circle the letter of the best answer.

1. Which of the following does the passage NOT discuss?

   a. the world's fastest dog

   b. the world's smallest dog

   c. a dog who saved a person's life

   d. the world's largest dog

2. According to the article, why do people have dogs as pets?

   a. Dogs used to live in caves.

   b. Dogs come in all shapes and sizes.

   c. Dogs are great companions.

   d. The passage doesn't say.

3. Which sentence about Zorba is true?

   a. He was taller and heavier than an adult man.

   b. He was taller, but not heavier than an adult man.

   c. He was heavier, but not taller than an adult man.

   d. He was neither heavier nor taller than an adult man.

4. According to the passage, the world's smallest dog weighed half as much as _____.

   a. a child's hand

   b. this book

   c. a matchbox

   d. Zorba

5. Which is NOT true about Allen Parton?

   a. His dog has been on TV.

   b. He received a medal for bravery.

   c. He is unable to walk.

   d. He has been in at least two car accidents.

Idioms

Find each idiom in the story.

1. **back and forth**—*from one side to another*
   - Whenever he's nervous he likes to walk **back and forth**.
   - The tennis players hit the ball **back and forth** for a long time.

2. **in comparison**—*compared to*
   - Sean looks really nervous. Ian, **in comparison**, looks very relaxed.
   - The amount of money we spend on food is minor **in comparison** with the amount of money we spend on rent.

3. **pass away**—*die (polite)*
   - I was sorry to hear that his father **passed away**.
   - Ellyn got married again three years after her husband **passed away**.

Vocabulary Reinforcement

A. Circle the letter of the word or phrase that best completes the sentence.

1. It took Brian almost six months to completely _____ from his illness.

   a. pass away   **b.** recover   **c.** cure   **d.** health

2. I saw a great _____ about Africa on TV last night.

   a. script   **b.** scenery   **c.** documentary   **d.** companion

3. It was so cold last night I needed to get an extra _____ for my bed.

   a. blanket   **b.** feather   **c.** runner-up   **d.** reward

4. Nathan gave a _____ to the person who found his wallet.

   a. palm   **b.** bunch   **c.** bravery   **d.** reward

5. Takako is sad because her mother _____ last year.

   a. recovered   **b.** passed away   **c.** made up   **d.** gained an understanding

6. That bus goes _____ between the downtown area and the airport.

   a. back and forth   **b.** get back   **c.** even though   **d.** in comparison

B. Complete the passage with items from the box. One item is extra.

documentary bravery wheelchair companion remarkable in comparison

Dogs are very popular pets, and they come in all shapes and sizes. Two of the most (1)_____ dogs were the largest dog in the world, Zorba, and the smallest dog, a Yorkshire terrier. Zorba weighed more than a person. (2)_____, the Yorkshire terrier could easily be picked up by a child. Another dog was famous not for its size, but for its (3)_____. This dog is the (4)_____ of a man who can't walk and has to use a (5)_____. It saved the man's life after he was hit by a car.

What Do You Think?

1. People say "a dog is a man's best friend." Do you think this is true? If not, what other animals are more important?

2. Why do people have pets? What are some reasons for and against having pets?

Diamonds

Before You Read

Answer the following questions.

1. Does anyone in your family have any diamonds, for example, a diamond ring?

   _____

   _____

2. How much would a diamond ring cost in your country?

   _____

   _____

3. What's the most expensive item you've ever seen?

   _____

   _____

To: James
From: Jesus

Target Vocabulary

Match each word with the best meaning.

1. _____ arrest
2. _____ disguise
3. _____ exhibition
4. _____ gang
5. _____ robbery
6. _____ security
7. _____ swap
8. _____ thief

a. change the way someone looks to trick other people

b. people or technology that keep buildings and other areas safe

c. an act of stealing

d. a robber; a person who steals

e. a group of people (often criminals)

f. capture and hold someone (by the police)

g. change one thing for another; exchange

h. a display or show (in an art gallery or museum)

Visitors to London's Millennium[1] Dome building on the morning of November 7, 2000 would have seen much more than they had expected. The Dome, a building which was built to celebrate the beginning of the new millennium, had a special display, called "Money," containing some of the world's most famous diamonds.

5 Shortly after opening time, four men **disguised** as workmen drove a large digging machine past **security** guards at the entrance. After coming near the **exhibition**, they put on gas masks and released smoke bombs.

Their target was The Millenium Star, a 203-carat perfect blue diamond, thought to be the most beautiful large diamond in the world, and the third largest ever 10 discovered.

Unfortunately for the **thieves**, the police had been keeping an eye on them for months, after seeing two **gang** members videotaping the diamonds two months earlier. As the thieves used hammers to break into the glass case containing the diamonds, police officers disguised as cleaners quickly surrounded and arrested 15 the men. The police had also **swapped** the diamonds for fakes[2] a few hours before the **robbery** attempt.

The gang had planned to get away by speedboat[3] along the river outside the exhibition. The two drivers of the boat were also **arrested** after a high-speed chase[4] along the river. If the robbery attempt had succeeded, it would have been 20 the largest in history—worth over $500 million. The thieves were given a total of seventy-one years in prison, with the two main leaders receiving eighteen years each.

Two years later, in February 2002, another gang of thieves succeeded in stealing millions of dollars' worth of diamonds in Antwerp, the diamond-dealing[5] city in 25 Belgium. They used copied keys and stolen security passes to get into the area containing the diamonds on Sunday night. The robbery wasn't discovered until Monday morning. The four thieves might have gotten away with the robbery, except for their carelessness—they were captured after they left a garbage bag containing security passes, videotapes, and documents with their names on the 30 side of a road.

_____ **minutes** _____ **seconds** (341 words)

> ### Did You Know?
>
> The world's largest diamond, the Cullinan, weighed 3,106 carats (about 600 g) when uncut. It was cut into nine major diamonds, and ninety-six minor ones, many of which are now part of the Crown Jewels in London.

---

[1] **millennium** a thousand years
[2] **fake** something that is not real or true
[3] **speedboat** a small fast boat
[4] **chase** follow someone very quickly
[5] **deal** trade; buy and sell

Reading Comprehension

Circle the letter of the best answer.

1. What is the best title for this passage?
   - **a.** The Most Famous Diamond
   - **b.** Diamond Robberies
   - **c.** Diamond Exhibitions
   - **d.** Successful Escapes

2. What did the Millennium robbers NOT do?
   - **a.** They tried to escape by boat.
   - **b.** They used security passes.
   - **c.** They broke the glass around the diamonds.
   - **d.** They used smoke bombs.

3. What did the police do at the Millennium Dome?
   - **a.** They videotaped the robbery.
   - **b.** They disguised themselves as security guards.
   - **c.** They swapped the diamonds for fakes.
   - **d.** They broke the glass around the diamonds.

4. Why didn't the Antwerp robbery succeed?
   - **a.** The robbers were careless.
   - **b.** The gang copied the wrong keys.
   - **c.** The police videotaped the robbers.
   - **d.** The police arrested the robbers on a boat.

5. What is similar about the two robberies?
   - **a.** They both succeeded.
   - **b.** They happened in the same city.
   - **c.** They both needed a lot of planning.
   - **d.** Both gangs of robbers planned to escape by boat.

Idioms

Find each idiom in the story.

1. **get away (with)**—*escape from somewhere; escape punishment for doing something bad*
   - The thieves **got away** with one million dollars' worth of gold.
   - He thought he had **gotten away**, but the police were waiting for him outside the bank.

2. **keep an eye on**—*watch*
   - Can you please **keep an eye on** my bag for a few minutes?
   - The store security guard **kept an eye on** the group of young girls.

3. **break into**—*enter a building or car by force*
   - Someone **broke into** Phil's house while he was away on vacation.
   - The police arrested the two men while they were **breaking into** a car parked on the street.

Vocabulary Reinforcement

A. Circle the letter of the word or phrase that best completes the sentence.

1. These days there is a lot more _____ at the airport than there used to be.
   a. disguise   **b.** fate   **c.** interest   **d.** security

2. There was a big _____ at the bank downtown last night.
   a. thief   **b.** robbery   **c.** capture   **d.** disguise

3. I hope the police catch the _____ who stole my car.
   a. robbery   **b.** arrest   **c.** thief   **d.** security

4. Paula shouted when she saw someone attempting to _____ her neighbor's house.
   a. break into   **b.** check into   **c.** watch out for   **d.** get back to

5. Three years after the robbery, the thieves were finally _____.
   a. disguised   **b.** arrested   **c.** passed away   **d.** gotten away with

6. Young people today think they can _____ anything.
   a. hand out   **b.** fall out of fashion   **c.** keep an eye on   **d.** get away with

B. Complete the passage with items from the box. One item is extra.

arrested	security	disguised	exhibition	keeping an eye on	gang

A (1)_____ of thieves tried to steal a huge famous diamond. The diamond was in a(n) (2)_____ in London's Millennium Dome. The thieves (3)_____ themselves as workmen to get to the diamond, but police officers were waiting, and quickly (4)_____ the thieves. The police had been (5)_____ them for many weeks before the robbery. The leaders of the robbers will have to stay in prison for eighteen years.

What Do You Think?

1. Why do you think that diamonds are so popular?
2. Have there been any famous robberies in your country? What happened to the criminals? Did they get away with it?

A. Find words for each definition. Two words are extra.

associate	blanket	companion	constant	experiment
order	represent	reward	runner-up	security	swap	unfortunately

1. _____ a scientific test
2. _____ unluckily; by bad luck
3. _____ show; mean; stand for; replace
4. _____ someone that goes or lives with another person; friend
5. _____ not changing
6. _____ a prize given for doing something good
7. _____ someone who comes in second in a contest or race
8. _____ a warm bed covering
9. _____ connect something in the mind
10. _____ change one thing for another; exchange

B. Complete the paragraph with items from the box. Two items are extra.

arrested	broke into	disguised	documentaries	got away with	thieves
kept an eye on	made up	passed away	recovered	remarkable	rewarded

One of the most famous robberies of the last century is The Great Train Robbery, which took place in England in 1963. At 3 A.M. on August 8th, a gang of fifteen men (1)_____ as railway workers stopped a night train carrying mail. The gang hit the train driver, Jack Mills, over the head, and (2)_____ the locked train. They (3)_____ 120 bags of cash, containing £2.6 million (worth about US$66 million today).

Due to the robbers' carelessness, the police quickly (4)_____ most of the gang, but one of the (5)_____, Ronald Biggs, escaped to South America, where he lived for many years. The English police (6)_____ him, but were unable to arrest him until he finally returned to England in 2001.

Jack Mills never (7)_____ from the injuries he received in the robbery, and (8)_____ in 1970. The (9)_____ story of this robbery has been the subject of quite a few (10)_____.

C. Match each idiom with the best definition. One definition is extra.

1. _____ back and forth
2. _____ be related to
3. _____ believe in
4. _____ by heart
5. _____ check in
6. _____ get back
7. _____ get over
8. _____ give something a try
9. _____ in comparison
10. _____ make up

a. attempt something for the first time
b. by memory
c. compared to
d. enter a hotel
e. from one side to another
f. get better after a sickness
g. have a connection to
h. invent
i. return
j. think that something is true or a good idea
k. watch

D. Use the clues below to complete the crossword.

Across

1. There was a bank _____ last week, and the thieves got away with $4 million.
4. big; important
5. a group of people (often criminals)
6. small; less important
7. a person who steals
9. a topic or subject that people are concerned about
11. a power that decides a person's future
14. I saw a great _____ at the museum today.
15. the inside part of your hand with lines on it
16. forever; never-ending
17. unplanned; happening at any place or any time
18. medicine or treatment that makes a person well again

12. At the newspaper, the journalists give their articles to the _____ before they are published.
13. I only have a little milk, but I think Sarah has _____. (3 words)

Down

1. a connection between people, ideas, or things
2. not being afraid of danger
3. Was it very _____ when you broke your arm?
8. That film was really _____. I couldn't stop laughing.
9. To write novels you'd need a great _____.
10. Since his accident, he can't walk and has to use a _____.

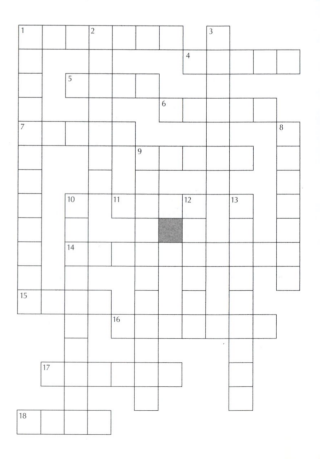

Space Explorers 16

Before You Read

Answer the following questions.

1. Do you remember any stories about space travel?

   _____

   _____

2. Do you know the names of any astronauts or spacecraft?

   _____

   _____

3. What do you think is the longest time that anyone has spent in space?

   _____

   _____

Target Vocabulary

Match each word with the best meaning.

1. _____ aboard
2. _____ astronaut
3. _____ (to) conduct
4. _____ launch
5. _____ mission
6. _____ predict
7. _____ rocket
8. _____ satellite

a. a long space vehicle

b. send up into the air, or into space

c. say what will happen in the future

d. a person who goes into space

e. organize and carry out

f. an object sent into space as part of a communication system

g. on a ship, train, plane, or other vehicle

h. an important job that a group of people are sent somewhere (usually another country) to do

After men landed on the moon in 1969, **astronauts** around the world had a problem—there were no other places they could go! Even today, the other planets are still too far away for astronauts to fly to. So, while **rockets** and robots[1] can go to other planets,[2] manned flights have to stay closer to home, for the time being.
5 Therefore, since visiting the moon, manned space programs have turned their attention to solving problems related to living and working in space.

Currently, NASA's[3] manned space exploration program focuses on the space shuttle program. NASA now operates three space shuttles, Discovery, Atlantis, and Endeavor. Unfortunately, two of NASA's shuttles, Challenger and Columbia,
10 have been lost through accidents. Seven astronauts died in each accident. Since the beginning of the shuttle program, the shuttles have flown more than a hundred **missions**. These missions have included putting **satellites** into orbit,[4] photographing the earth, studying space, **conducting** experiments related to working in space, and connecting with various manned space stations in orbit.

15 Throughout the short history of the exploration of space, several space stations have been put into orbit. The first manned space station was the Soviet station Salyut 1, put into orbit in 1971. Later, in 1986, the Soviet Union **launched** the Mir space station. Mir stayed in orbit until March 23, 2001. Over that time, 104 astronauts visited the station to stay for various lengths of time. The person who
20 has spent the longest in space so far is Russian astronaut Valeri Polyakov. Working as the doctor **aboard** the station, he lived on Mir for 438 days without returning to earth. In total, Polyakov worked aboard Mir for 678 days before retiring.

25 Today, astronauts from around the world are working together to complete the International Space Station (ISS). The first part of this space station was launched in 1998. NASA **predicts** the ISS should be completed by 2011. In the
30 long run, it is hoped that the ISS will be a place where people can live and work all year round.

_____ **minutes** _____ **seconds** (339 words)

[1] **robot** a machine, often shaped like a person, which can be programmed to do different things
[2] **planet** a large round object in space that moves around a star, e.g., Earth, Mars, and Venus
[3] **NASA** National Aeronautics and Space Administration, the space exploration organization for the United States
[4] **orbit** a path in space around another object (in this case, Earth)

Reading Comprehension

Circle the letter of the best answer.

1. What is the best title for this passage?

   a. Valeri Polyakov—An Amazing Astronaut

   b. The Past and Future of Space Travel

   c. Space Cities of the Future

   d. Living and Working on the International Space Station

2. Why can't astronauts travel to other planets now?

   a. There are not enough space shuttles.

   b. There have been too many rocket accidents.

   c. There are too many problems here on Earth.

   d. The journey would take too long for a person.

3. How many space shuttle astronauts have been killed in accidents?

   a. 2

   b. 7

   c. 14

   d. 100

4. What is NOT true about Valeri Polyakov?

   a. He is a doctor.

   b. He stayed aboard Mir for 678 days at one time.

   c. He is not an astronaut any more.

   d. He has spent more time in space than anyone else.

5. What is true about the International Space Station?

   a. It is being built by the United States alone.

   b. It will be launched into space in 2011.

   c. It was completed in 1998.

   d. It will eventually have people living and working there all the time.

Idioms

Find each idiom in the story.

1. **for the time being**—*for now, but only until something else becomes possible*
   - I need a new car, but **for the time being** I'll have to keep my old one.
   - The fighting between the two countries has stopped **for the time being**.

2. **in the long run**—*over a long period of time into the future*
   - The price of houses always seems to increase **in the long run**.
   - Smoking is very bad for your health **in the long run**.

3. **so far**—*until now*
   - I love traveling. **So far**, I've been to fifty-three countries.
   - That mountain is very dangerous. **So far**, no one has been able to climb it.

Vocabulary Reinforcement

A. Circle the letter of the word or phrase that best completes the sentence.

1. I've been studying all morning, but _____ I've only memorized fifteen words.
   a. by heart   b. so far   c. in the long run   d. for the time being

2. Maria would love to retire, but she needs the money, so _____ she has to keep working.
   a. even though   b. so far   c. for one thing   d. for the time being

3. He's a great fortune-teller. Everything he _____ comes true.
   a. conducts   b. recovers   c. captures   d. predicts

4. The President sent a team of experts on an important _____ to try to end the war.
   a. satellite   b. documentary   c. mission   d. security

5. This car is very expensive, but it will drive well for many years, and _____ you will save money.
   a. in the long run   b. so far   c. even though   d. for the time being

6. NASA put an expensive communications _____ into orbit last week.
   a. robot   b. astronaut   c. satellite   d. planet

B. Complete the passage with items from the box. One item is extra.

aboard	astronauts	rocket	conduct	launched	predicted

It is not yet possible for people to travel to other planets by (1)_____ because the planets are so far away. Therefore, manned space programs today focus on developing safe ways for (2)_____ to live and work in space. One way space programs can (3)_____ experiments on living and working in space is by putting space stations in orbit. The Russian space station Mir was (4)_____ into orbit in 1986, and it stayed up for more than ten years. One astronaut lived (5)_____ Mir for 438 days without returning to Earth!

What Do You Think?

1. Would you like to live on the International Space Station? How long do you think you could live there?

2. Why do you think that people are so interested in space travel?

Happy New Year!

Before You Read

Answer the following questions.

1. What do people do to celebrate New Year in your country? _____

2. What did you do last New Year? _____

3. Do you know of any New Year customs in other countries? _____

Target Vocabulary

Match each word with the best meaning.

1. _____ calendar
2. _____ doll
3. _____ evening
4. _____ gown
5. _____ habit
6. _____ prefer
7. _____ promise
8. _____ widespread

a. a way to show days, weeks, and months in a year
b. like more
c. say you will do something
d. a toy that looks like a person
e. the period between about 6 P.M. and midnight
f. a long formal dress
g. something someone does often
h. common; found or happening in many places

Almost all cultures celebrate the end of one year and the beginning of another in some way. Different cultures celebrate the beginning of a new year in different ways, and at different times on the **calendar**.

5 In Western countries, people usually celebrate New Year at midnight on January 1st. People may go to parties, dress in formal clothes—like tuxedos[1] and **evening gowns**, and drink champagne at midnight. During the first minutes of the new year, people cheer and wish each other happiness for the year ahead. But
10 some cultures **prefer** to celebrate the new year by waking up early to watch the sun rise. They welcome the new year with the first light of the sunrise.

It is also a common Western custom to make a New Year's **promise**, called a resolution. New Year's
15 resolutions usually include promises to try something new or change a bad **habit** in the new year.

Many cultures also do special things to get rid of bad luck at the beginning of a new year. For example, in Ecuador, families make a big **doll** from old clothes. The doll is filled with old newspapers and firecrackers. At midnight, these dolls are
20 burned to show the bad things from the past year are gone and the new year can start afresh. Other common traditions to keep away bad luck in a new year include throwing things into rivers or the ocean, or saying special things on the first day of the new year.

Other New Year traditions are followed to bring good luck in the new year. A
25 **widespread** Spanish tradition for good luck is to eat grapes on New Year's Day. The more grapes a person eats, the more good luck the person will have in the year. In France, people eat pancakes for good luck at New Year. In the United States, some people eat black-eyed peas[2] for good luck—but to get good luck for a whole year you have to eat 365 of them!

_____ **minutes** _____ **seconds** (333 words)

> ### Did You Know?
> According to many surveys, the most common New Year's resolutions every year are: lose weight, get more exercise, save money, and stop smoking.

---

[1] **tuxedo** a type of suit worn to formal occasions
[2] **black-eyed pea** a small, round, bean-like vegetable that has a large black spot; commonly used in southern U.S. cooking

Reading Comprehension

Circle the letter of the best answer.

1. What is the main idea of the reading?

   a. the meaning of "Happy New Year!"

   b. what date New Year is celebrated in different cultures

   c. various New Year traditions

   d. why people make resolutions

2. Which culture celebrates New Year in the morning?

   a. the United States

   b. Spain

   c. France

   d. The passage doesn't say.

3. What is a resolution?

   a. something you burn

   b. something you eat

   c. something you say

   d. something you wear

4. What is the topic of the fourth paragraph?

   a. bringing good luck

   b. keeping away bad luck

   c. planning for the next year

   d. remembering the past

5. Which is probably true about eating black-eyed peas on New Year?

   a. Black-eyed peas taste bad.

   b. One pea brings one day of luck.

   c. The peas are very difficult to cook.

   d. It is bad luck to eat a lot of black-eyed peas.

Idioms

Find each idiom in the story.

1. **get rid of**—*throw away; not keep*
   - I want to **get rid of** all of these old clothes that I never wear.
   - She **got rid of** her old car and bought a motorbike.

2. **keep away**—*make something stay far away*
   - **Keep away** from the stove! It's hot!
   - Put on this cream. It will **keep away** the mosquitoes.

3. **start afresh**—*start again from the beginning*
   - I didn't like what I had written, so I **started afresh**.
   - The dog ate Michelle's cake, so she had to **start afresh**.

Vocabulary Reinforcement

A. Circle the letter of the word or phrase that best completes the sentence.

1. Young children should _____ the swimming pool when no adults are there.
   a. get rid of   **b.** keep away from   **c.** break into   **d.** keep an eye on

2. It's already a new month! I need to turn over my _____.
   a. calendar   **b.** habit   **c.** gown   **d.** resolution

3. Please _____ you won't tell anyone my secret.
   a. prefer   **b.** disguise   **c.** argue   **d.** promise

4. Some people think that smoking is a terrible _____.
   a. habit   **b.** fate   **c.** resolution   **d.** explosive

5. That disease is very _____ in Africa, and kills millions of people every year.
   a. rare   **b.** formal   **c.** brave   **d.** widespread

6. Max bought his daughter a _____ for her birthday.
   a. tuxedo   **b.** satellite   **c.** doll   **d.** mission

B. Complete the passage with items from the box. One item is extra.

get rid of	prefer	promises	gowns	start afresh	evening

New Year is celebrated around the world through many different customs. In Western
countries, many people go to parties in the (1)_____ wearing formal clothes, like
tuxedos and (2)_____. In other cultures, people (3)_____ to get up early
and watch the sun rise. Many cultures also have New Year traditions to (4)_____
bad luck and (5)_____ in the new year.

What Do You Think?

1. If you had to make a New Year's resolution, what would it be? Why?
2. What's your favorite public holiday? Why?

Text Messaging

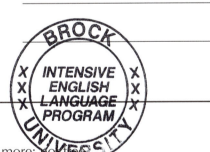

[Text message display reads: "My smmr hols wr CWOT. B4, we usd 2go2 NY 2C my bro, his GF & 3 kds FTF."]

Before You Read

Answer the following questions.

1. Do you have a cell phone?
   If yes, how often do you use it?
   _____

2. Do you or your friends ever send text messages?
   _____

3. Look at the text message above.
   What do you think it means?
   _____

Target Vocabulary

Match each word with the best meaning.

1. _____ characteristic
2. _____ comfortable
3. _____ essay
4. _____ expert
5. _____ in particular
6. _____ limited
7. _____ technology
8. _____ evolve

a. restricted; not allowed to be more; not free
b. especially
c. change or develop over time
d. modern machines or equipment
e. a short piece of writing on a topic, showing the author's opinion
f. person who knows a lot about, and understands, a subject
g. giving a relaxed feeling; easy
h. feature or quality of something that makes it recognizable or special

Can you understand the beginning of this **essay?**

"My smmr hols wr CWOT. B4, we usd 2go2 NY 2C my bro, his GF & 3 kds FTF."

The Scottish teacher who received it in class had
5   no idea what the girl who wrote it meant. The
essay was written in a form of English used in cell
phone[1] text messages. Text messages (also called
SMS[2]) through cell phones became very popular in
the late 1990s. At first, mobile phone companies
10 thought that text messaging would be a good way
to send messages to customers, but customers
quickly began to use the text messaging service to
send messages to each other. Teenagers **in
particular** enjoyed using text messaging, and they began to create a new language
15 for messages called *texting*.

A text message is **limited** to 160 characters, including letters, spaces, and
numbers, so messages must be kept short. In addition, typing on the small keypad
of a cell phone is difficult, so it's common to make words shorter. In texting, a
single letter or number can represent a word, like "r" for "are," "u" for "you,"
20 and "2" for "to." Several letters can also represent a phrase, like "lol" for
"laughing out loud." Another **characteristic** of texting is the leaving out of letters
in a word, like spelling "please" as "pls."

Some parents and teachers worry that texting will make children bad spellers and
bad writers. The student who wrote the essay at the top of this page said writing
25 that way was more **comfortable** for her. (The essay said, "My summer holidays
were a complete waste of time. Before, we used to go to New York to see my
brother, his girlfriend, and their three kids face to face.")

Not everyone agrees that texting is a bad thing. Some **experts** say languages
always **evolve,** and this is just another way for English to change. Other people
30 believe texting will disappear soon. New **technology** for voice messages may soon
make text messages a thing of the past.

 _____ **minutes** _____ **seconds** (336 words)

Did You Know?
Text messages have been used to save a number of people's lives, including an Australian woman lost in the desert, and a German snowboarder trapped in the snow.

---

[1] **cell phone** a mobile phone
[2] **SMS** Short Message Service

Reading Comprehension

Circle the letter of the best answer.

1. What is the writer's opinion of text messaging?

   a. It is fun and easy to do.

   b. It is not bad for children.

   c. It will make children bad writers.

   d. The writer does not give an opinion.

2. Which characteristic of texting is NOT described in the passage?

   a. using letters to represent words

   b. using numbers to represent words

   c. using letters to represent phrases

   d. using phrases to represent essays

3. Which of the following was most probably the title of the student's essay?

   a. My Gr8 Tchr

   b. CU in LA

   c. My GF

   d. My Smmr Hols

4. Why do some people think that texting is bad?

   a. It costs too much.

   b. It's too difficult to type.

   c. Children won't learn to write correctly.

   d. It's not comfortable.

5. Why aren't some people worried about the effect of texting?

   a. Not many people use texting.

   b. Spelling in English is too difficult.

   c. Children quickly become bored with texting.

   d. Texting will disappear because of new technology.

Idioms

Find each idiom in the story.

1. **face to face**—*directly; in person*
   - I want to hear her say that to me **face to face**.
   - He looked forward to meeting his pen friend **face to face**.

2. **out loud**—*spoken aloud, not silently*
   - She thought of a good idea, but she was afraid to say it **out loud**.
   - He read his poem **out loud** for the audience.

3. **a waste of time/money**—*not a good use of time or money*
   - Don't go see that movie. It's **a waste of time**.
   - The exercise bike was **a waste of money**. No one ever used it.

Vocabulary Reinforcement

A. Circle the letter of the word or phrase that best completes the sentence.

1. All the movies at the film festival look good, but there is one _____ I really want to see.

   a. in the long run **b.** limited **c.** waste of time **d.** in particular

2. Please read your essay _____ for the class.

   a. face to face **b.** out loud **c.** for the time being **d.** in comparison

3. The sofa was so _____ that I quickly fell asleep.

   a. comfortable **b.** amusing **c.** annual **d.** evolved

4. Over many millions of years, dinosaurs _____ into birds and other animals.

   a. translated **b.** evolved **c.** recovered **d.** started afresh

5. I don't want to talk to her over the phone. We need to meet _____.

   a. out loud **b.** back and forth **c.** on the other hand **d.** face to face

6. On my trip to Sri Lanka, I learned an interesting _____ for catching fish.

   a. conduct **b.** technology **c.** robot **d.** technique

B. Complete the passage with items from the box. One item is extra.

technology	a technique	limited	experts	a waste of time	an essay

Texting is a way to write short messages on mobile phones. The messages are (1)_____ to 160 characters, so writers use one letter or several letters to represent words or phrases. One student wrote (2)_____ using texting, which worried her teacher. Some people worry that children will become bad writers. However, other language (3)_____ say it is (4)_____ to worry because English is evolving naturally, and also, soon new (5)_____ will come up with alternatives to texting.

What Do You Think?

1. Do you think that text messaging causes "bad" English? Why or why not?
2. Do you think that your language is changing over time? If yes, how?

Urban Legends

Before You Read

Answer the following questions.

1. Have you ever heard a story you thought was true, but which turned out to be false?

   _____

   _____

2. Are there any famous stories from long ago in your country? Do you know if there is any truth in them?

   _____

   _____

3. What is the most unusual true story you have ever heard?

   _____

   _____

Target Vocabulary

Match each word with the best meaning.

1. _____ bizarre
2. _____ legend
3. _____ obvious
4. _____ shrink
5. _____ threaten
6. _____ urban
7. _____ version
8. _____ victim

a. easy and clear to see and understand

b. very strange or unusual

c. become smaller

d. say you will do something bad if someone doesn't do what you want

e. related to a city

f. a story or myth, usually from long ago

g. someone who has been hurt or killed by someone or something

h. a particular form of something that is similar but not the same as earlier and later forms

Have you heard about the woman who put her wet dog in the microwave to dry it, and ended up cooking her dog by mistake? Or did you hear about the man who died
5 at his desk at work, and nobody in the office noticed he was dead for five days? These stories have two things in common. They are both not true, and they are both **urban legends**.

10 Usually, legends are stories of events from long ago. Urban legends, on the other hand, are stories set in the recent past, perhaps even last week! Urban legends also take place in cities or in places well known
15 to people. Another characteristic of urban legends is that there are many different **versions** of the same story, with local information changed to make the story seem more real. Today, the Internet has become a common way for urban legends to spread very quickly.

A good example of an urban legend is the story of the girl who was killed by
20 her jeans. In the 1980s, it was fashionable to wear very tight jeans. At that time, Levi's sold special jeans that **shrank** when you washed them. According to the story, a teenage girl wanted to make her jeans as tight as possible, so she wore them in the bathtub. Unfortunately, they shrank so much that the girl died! Actually, this legend started from a Levi's advertisement on television. In the TV
25 ad, a man stepped into a bathtub and his tight jeans became the perfect size. The popularity of this legend **obviously** comes from the idea of teens trying too hard to look good.

However, some stories that sound like urban legends actually start from **bizarre** real events. For example, there is a story about muggers[1] using snakes to rob
30 people. There have been real reports about muggers doing this. The muggers **threaten** a **victim** by holding a snake in the person's face. Then the robber takes the victim's money. According to legend, these robbers are very common, so you should keep an eye out for strangers carrying snakes.

_____ **minutes** _____ **seconds** (348 words)

Did You Know?

Some urban legends are very old—one, about a murderer who hides in the back seat of a car, was first reported in the early 1800s, when people used horse-drawn carriages.

---

[1] **mugger** a thief who attacks people for their money, often on a city street

Reading Comprehension

Circle the letter of the best answer.

1. What is the best title for this passage?

   a. Amazing True Stories   **c.** Bizarre Crimes

   b. Legends through History   **d.** Bizarre Stories

2. What is NOT true about urban legends?

   a. They usually take place in the country, or in small towns.

   b. There is usually more than one version of the legend.

   c. They are sometimes based on a real event.

   d. The Internet has made urban legends more widespread.

3. What happened to the girl in the jeans story?

   a. She shrank.   **c.** Her jeans became too small.

   b. She starred in a television commercial. **d.** A man stepped into her bathtub.

4. According to the passage, why do some muggers use snakes?

   a. Snakes are very common.   **c.** Snakes are very dangerous.

   b. Everyone is scared of snakes.   **d.** The passage doesn't say.

5. Which story in the passage really happened?

   a. The dog in the microwave.   **c.** The girl who was killed by her jeans.

   b. The dead man in the office.   **d.** The muggers who threaten victims
                                                with snakes.

Idioms

Find each idiom in the story.

1. **have (something) in common (with)**—*share a feature or characteristic*
   - The reason that Brooke and her boyfriend have such a good relationship is because they **have** so much **in common**.
   - The only thing the students in this class **have in common** is their need to learn English.

2. **keep an eye out for**—*watch for something carefully*
   - Whenever I'm in a bookstore, I **keep an eye out for** interesting new books.
   - There have been quite a few robberies in our neighborhood, so **keep an eye out for** strange people.

3. **hear about**—*learn about, hear a story about*
   - How did you **hear about** this restaurant?
   - Clifford was scared after he **heard about** the muggers in the area.

Vocabulary Reinforcement

A. Circle the letter of the word or phrase that best completes the sentence.

1. There is a traditional Japanese _____ about *Momotaro,* the Peach Boy.
   a. article   **b.** essay   **c.** legend   **d.** urban

2. That question on the test was too easy. The answer was _____ to everyone.
   a. obvious   **b.** complicated   **c.** bizarre   **d.** random

3. Harvey _____ to quit his job if he didn't get a pay increase.
   a. evolved   **b.** threatened   **c.** launched   **d.** limited

4. When you're at the shopping mall today, _____ any bargains.
   a. keep your eye on   **b.** hear about   **c.** break into   **d.** keep an eye out for

5. In many countries, people are leaving farms and moving to _____ areas.
   a. urban   **b.** obvious   **c.** widespread   **d.** common

6. The robber was caught, and the money was returned to the _____.
   a. mugger   **b.** victim   **c.** thief   **d.** blanket

B. Complete the passage with items from the box. One item is extra.

bizarre	victims	in common	heard about	shrank	versions

If you have (1)_____ the woman who died because her jeans (2)_____
too much, then you have heard an urban legend. Most urban legends have several
characteristics (3)_____: there are usually several different (4)_____ of
the same story; they often take place in urban areas; and because they sound
(5)_____, but not obviously untrue, many people believe them completely.

What Do You Think?

1. Would you have believed any of the untrue stories mentioned in the reading? Which do you think was the most believable?

2. Do you think most of what you read on the Internet is true? What kinds of online information do you think you can trust the most, and the least?

Extreme Sports

Before You Read

Answer the following questions.

1. Do you like to watch sports on TV? If yes, what sports do you like to watch? _____

2. Which sports do you like to play or do? _____

3. Are there any sports that you would never try? Why? _____

Target Vocabulary

Match each word with the best meaning.

1. _____ athlete
2. _____ convince
3. _____ demonstrate
4. _____ encourage
5. _____ extreme
6. _____ junior
7. _____ organize
8. _____ tour

a. arrange; plan; set up

b. far from normal; far from the center

c. younger

d. show how to do something

e. a vacation or trip that includes many different places

f. a person who does or plays a sport

g. make others believe that something is true or a good idea

h. give strength or hope to someone; help someone to do something

In the summer of 1993, Ron Semaio, director of programming for the U.S. sports cable channel ESPN, came up with an idea for a new sports program. While he was watching television one afternoon, Semaio started to think about how much young people liked to do **extreme** sports, like skateboarding, snowboarding, and
5 BMX bike riding. He thought of an event where people could watch **athletes** compete in these sports in a kind of extreme Olympics.

It took some time to **convince** the management at ESPN that the idea showed promise, and then it took even longer to
10 **organize** the competition. Finally, in the summer of 1995, the first Extreme Games took place in Rhode Island in the United States. More than 350 athletes from around the world came to compete in events such as
15 bungee jumping, barefoot waterskiing, windsurfing, BMX biking, skateboarding, and climbing. The competitions were shown on ESPN and were a big hit, especially with males between twelve and thirty years old.

20 The success of the first show resulted in the competition becoming an annual event. The second year, ESPN renamed the competition the X Games. The organizers also announced that they would hold a winter X Games that year. In the winter games, athletes competed in BMX racing on snow,
25 snowboarding, ice climbing, and various ski competitions.

That same year, a few athletes were also asked to travel to Brazil and China to **demonstrate** their skill and to stir up interest in the X Games in those countries. The **touring** X Games show became known as the X Trials. New athletes could compete in the X Trials, and if they did well, they were then allowed to compete
30 in the X Games. In addition to the X Games held in the United States each year, there are also the Asian X Games, a Latin X Games, and a **Junior** X Games to **encourage** young athletes to compete in extreme sports.

_____ **minutes** _____ **seconds** (323 words)

Did You Know?

Hundreds of years ago, men on Pentecost Island in the South Pacific proved their bravery by tying vines to their feet and jumping from 30-meter towers. They were the world's first bungee jumpers.

Reading Comprehension

Circle the letter of the best answer.

1. What is the main topic of the reading?

    a. the life of Ron Semaio

    b. famous athletes in extreme sports

    c. the dangers of extreme sports

    d. the history of the X Games

2. Where did the first Extreme Games take place?

    a. Brazil

    b. the United States

    c. China

    d. The article doesn't say.

3. Which group was probably the largest group watching the first X Games?

    a. young men

    b. teenage girls

    c. men over thirty

    d. women in their twenties

4. Which was held first?

    a. Junior X Games

    b. Summer X Games

    c. Winter X Games

    d. the Extreme Games

5. In which paragraph does the writer describe how the X Games first became popular?

    a. paragraph 1

    b. paragraph 2

    c. paragraph 3

    d. paragraph 4

Idioms

Find each idiom in the story.

1. **result in**—*cause; lead to*
    • The heavy snow **resulted in** the school closing for the day.
    • Your bad diet will surely **result in** health problems in the future.

2. **stir up**—*excite*
    • The speaker **stirred up** the emotions of the crowd.
    • He is always trying to **stir up** trouble. The boss should fire him.

3. **show promise**—*seem like one will be good or successful in the future*
    • Jacqueline has just started playing the piano, but she already **shows promise**.
    • I didn't **show** any **promise** at soccer, so I gave it up.

Vocabulary Reinforcement

A. Circle the letter of the word or phrase that best completes the sentence.

1. He _____ his skill at walking on his hands.

    a. demonstrated   **b.** encouraged   **c.** organized   **d.** convinced

2. Alice didn't want to come to the party, but I managed to _____ her.

    a. threaten   **b.** shrink   **c.** organize   **d.** convince

3. The reason Fiona is so good at sports is because her parents really _____ her when she was young.

    a. demonstrated   **b.** experimented   **c.** launched   **d.** encouraged

4. I could never be _____—I don't like exercise.

    a. an author   **b.** an athlete   **c.** a robot   **d.** a junior

5. His friends are _____ a surprise party for him.

    a. organizing   **b.** inviting   **c.** convincing   **d.** limiting

6. Violet is going on a twelve-day _____ of Europe.

    a. resolution   **b.** period   **c.** tour   **d.** companion

B. Complete the passage with items from the box. One item is extra.

stir up	result in	extreme	show promise	convince	junior

The X Games are a competition for athletes in (1)_____ sports. In addition to the X Games, and the (2)_____ X Games (for younger athletes), there is also the X Trials, where competitors in the X Games travel to other countries to (3)_____ interest in the competition. If athletes (4)_____ in the X Trials, this might (5)_____ them going on to compete in the X Games.

What Do You Think?

1. How popular in your country are the sports mentioned in the reading?
2. If you had to organize an X Games in your country, what sports would you include? Would you like to take part?

Review 16-20

A. Find words for each definition. Two words are extra.

> characteristic   comfortable   convince   evolve   expert
> legend   obvious   predict   promise   version   victim   widespread

1. _____ say what will happen in the future
2. _____ change or develop over time
3. _____ say you will do something
4. _____ easy and clear to see and understand
5. _____ common; found or happening in many places
6. _____ someone who has been hurt or killed by someone or something
7. _____ feature or quality that makes someone or something recognizable or special
8. _____ a particular form of something that is similar, but not the same as, earlier and later forms
9. _____ giving a relaxed feeling
10. _____ make others believe that something is true

B. Complete the paragraph with items from the box. Two items are extra.

> a waste of money   astronaut   conduct   for the time being   in particular
> launched   limited to   missions   resulted in   rocket   so far   technology

People have been interested in the planet Mars since ancient times. Because of the distance of Mars from Earth, sending a manned (1)_____ to the planet isn't possible today. (2)_____, exploration of Mars is (3)_____ unmanned spaceships.

There have been several spaceships which have flown past Mars and sent photos back to Earth, but (4)_____ only a few have actually landed on the surface. The most famous of these (5)_____ was the Mars Pathfinder, which (6)_____ in 1996 and landed on Mars in 1997. The Pathfinder, which was like a robot car, was able to (7)_____ a lot of useful research before it stopped working.

Some people think that space exploration and, (8)_____, sending spaceships to other planets, is (9)_____. However, others think that the (10)_____ that is created, and the information that is learned, is good for all people.

C. Match each idiom with the best definition. One definition is extra.

1. _____ face to face
2. _____ get rid of
3. _____ have (something) in common
4. _____ hear about
5. _____ in the long run
6. _____ keep an eye out for
7. _____ keep away
8. _____ out loud
9. _____ show promise
10. _____ start afresh

a. cause; lead to
b. directly; in person
c. learn about; hear a story about
d. make something stay far away
e. over a long period of time into the future
f. seem like one will be good or successful in the future
g. share a feature or characteristic
h. spoken aloud; not silently
i. start again from the beginning
j. throw away; not keep
k. watch for something carefully

D. Use the clues below to complete the crossword.

Across

1. Many people think that smoking is a bad _____.
6. a long formal dress
7. younger
9. Could you please _____ how to use this machine for me?
13. an object sent into space as part of a communication system
14. Joanne has great parents. They always _____ her to do what makes her happy.
18. related to a city
19. I like rock music a little, but I _____ jazz.
20. make plans; arrange

Down

2. The ship left as soon as everyone was _____.
3. Next year Michele is going on a three-week _____ of South America.
4. say that you will hurt someone if they don't do what you want
5. very unusual
8. a toy that looks like a person
10. far from normal; far from the center
11. excite (2 words)
12. a person who goes into space
15. I have a _____ on my desk so I know what date it is.

16. To be a top _____ you need to train hard every day.
17. become smaller

World Map

Countries and places mentioned in the readings:

Europe

1. Belgium
2. Antwerp
3. England
4. London
5. Wimbledon
6. France
7. Germany
8. Italy
9. Portugal
10. Russia
11. Scotland
12. Sweden
13. Turkey
14. Istanbul

Asia/Australasia

15. Australia
16. Bangladesh
17. China
18. Hong Kong
19. India
20. Mumbai
21. Japan
22. Malaysia
23. Saudi Arabia
24. United Arab Emirates
25. Dubai
26. Pentecost Island

North America

27. Puerto Rico
28. The United States of America
29. California
30. Hollywood
31. New York
32. Rhode Island
33. Seattle

South America

34. Brazil
35. Ecuador

Vocabulary Index

Words and phrases included in the Target Vocabulary and Idioms sections are listed below. The number refers to the Unit in which the word or phrase first appears. Idioms are shown in *italics*.

A

a close call 6
a waste of time/money 18
aboard 16
achievement 2
adventure 9
afraid 2
aim 10
alternative 3
amusing 11
announcement 10
annual 10
argue 7
arrange 7
arrest 15
article 5
as a matter of fact 4
as a rule 6
associate (something with something) 13
astronaut 16
athlete 20
atmosphere 4
author 5

B

back and forth 14
basket 8
be into something 3
be related to 12
believe in 12
bizarre 19
blanket 14
bravery 14
break into 15
breathe 6
bride 7
bunch 8

by hand 9
by heart 13

C

calendar 17
career 2
carry on 10
casual 4
catch on 3
catch one's eye 4
category 10
ceremony 7
channel 3
characteristic 18
check in(to)/out (of) 11
comfortable 18
companion 14
compare 9
complicated 7
(to) conduct 16
constant 13
content 3
convince 20
costume 9
create 4
cure 11
custom 8

D

decrease 8
demonstrate 20
despite 2
determination 2
determine 1
disease 11
disguise 15
documentary 14
doll 17
downtown 4

E

editor 11
encourage 20
equipment 3
essay 18
estimate 1
eternal 13
even though 5
evening 17
eventually 5
evolve 18
exhibition 15
experiment 11
expert 18
explorer 5
explosive 10
export 6
extreme 20

F

face to face 18
fall out of fashion 8
fate 12
feather 8
for good 7
for one thing 9
for the time being 16
(to) found (something) 10

G

gain an understanding 4
gang 15
get away (with) 15
get back 11
get over 11
get rid of 17
give (something) a try 13
gown 17
groom 7

Author's Acknowledgments

I would like to acknowledge Ki Chul Kang for his inspiration and guidance. I would also like to acknowledge Ji Eun Jung for her honest feedback from the student perspective. Finally, I have to acknowledge all of those students who inspired me to seek out materials to suit the interest of a variety of readers. It was both enjoyable and instructive for me as a teacher and a writer.

I am also grateful to the following teaching professionals who gave very useful feedback as the second edition was being developed.

Casey Malarcher

Andrew White	Induk Institute of Technology, Seoul, South Korea
Chris Campbell	Congress Institute, Osaka, Japan
Claudia Sasía	Instituto México, Puebla, México
Corina Correa	ALUMNI, São Paulo, Brasil
Evelyn Shiang	Tung Nan Institute of Technology, Taipei, Taiwan
Gail Wu	Overseas Chinese Institute of Technology, Taichung, Taiwan
Iain B.M. Lambert	Tokyo Denki University, Tokyo, Japan
Jaeman Choi	Wonkwang University, Chollabukdo, South Korea
Karen Ku	Overseas Chinese Institute of Technology, Taichung, Taiwan
Lex Kim	Lex Kim English School, Seoul, South Korea
Lucila Sotomayor	Instituto D'Amicis, Puebla, México
Marlene Tavares de Almeida	WordShop, Belo Horizonte, Brasil
Pai Sung-Yeon	Charlie's International School, Seoul, South Korea
Pauline Kao	Tung Nan Institute of Technology, Taipei, Taiwan
Richmond Stroupe	World Language Center, Soka University, Tokyo, Japan
Robert McLeod	Kang's Language School, Seoul, South Korea
Sherri Lynn Leibert	Congress Institute, Tokyo, Japan
Shwu Hui Tsai	Chung Kuo Institute of Technology, Taipei, Taiwan
Taming Hsiung	Chung Kuo Institute of Technology, Taipei, Taiwan